Crisis in World Communism

Marxism in Search of Efficiency

CRISIS
IN
WORLD
COMMUNISM

MARXISM IN SEARCH OF EFFICIENCY

Frank O'Brien

THE FREE PRESS, *New York*
COLLIER-MACMILLAN LIMITED, *London*

For information, address:

THE FREE PRESS
A DIVISION OF THE MACMILLAN COMPANY
60 Fifth Avenue, New York, N. Y. 10011

Collier-Macmillan Canada, Ltd., Toronto, Ontario

and

The Committee for Economic Development
711 Fifth Avenue, New York, N. Y. 10022

Library of Congress Catalog Card Number: 65-16439

A Supplementary Paper

This Supplementary Paper is published by the Research and Policy Committee of the Committee for Economic Development in conformity with the CED Bylaws (Art. V, Sec. 6), which authorize the publication of a manuscript as a Supplementary Paper if:

a) It is recommended for publication by the Research Director because in his opinion, it "constitutes an important contribution to the understanding of a problem on which research has been initiated by the Research and Policy Committee" and,

b) It is approved for publication by a majority of an Editorial Board on the ground that it presents "an analysis which is a significant contribution to the understanding of the problem in question."

This Supplementary Paper relates to various policy statements previously published by the Research and Policy Committee concerning international economic problems.

The Editorial Board authorizing publication of this Supplementary Paper is composed of:

Howard C. Petersen	*Members of the Research and Policy Committee*
William Benton	*of the Committee for Economic Development*
Theodore W. Schultz	*Members of the Research Advisory Board*
Neil H. Jacoby	*of the Committee for Economic Development*
Alfred C. Neal	*President*
	of the Committee for Economic Development
Herbert Stein	*Director of Research of the Committee*
	for Economic Development

While publication of this Supplementary Paper is authorized by CED's by-laws, except as noted above, its contents have not been approved, disapproved, or acted upon by the Committee for Economic Development, the Board of Trustees, the Research and Policy Committee, the Research Advisory Board, the Research Staff, or any member of any board or committee, or any officer of the Committee for Economic Development.

"The analysis of the world situation at the beginning of the Sixties can only evoke in every fighter in the great communist movement feelings of profound satisfaction and legitimate pride. Indeed, comrades, life has greatly surpassed even the boldest and most optimistic predictions and expectations. Once it was customary to say that history was working for socialism; at the same time, one remembered that mankind would dump capitalism and that socialism would be victorious. Today, it is possible to assert that socialism is working for history, for the basic content of the contemporary historical process constitutes the establishment and consolidation of socialism on an international scale."

N. S. Khrushchov to the Communist Party of the Soviet Union, January 6, 1961

Contents

Acknowledgments

Thanks for editorial comment on an early draft are due to Messrs. William B. King, William W. Fulmer, Douglas C. and Oscar H. Hornig, and Gene F. Caprio. I received valuable editorial comment on a late draft from Sterling F. Green.

Mr. Herbert Stein, Research Director of CED, gave me editorial help, and advice on the subject matter, with respect to several early and late drafts. I owe him thanks for this assistance, and for his patience with the interruptions in the work of his staff occasioned by production of the book.

I have a particular debt of gratitude to three specialists on Soviet economic policy who were good enough to read the study and give me detailed criticism: Professor Alec Nove, University of Glascow; Dr. Gregory Grossman, University of California at Berkeley, and Dr. Leon M. Herman, Legislative Reference Service, Library of Congress, Washington, D.C.

I have tried to profit from the advice of all the above. None, however, bears any responsibility for the contents of the study, or for its outlook.

Mr. Seong H. Park undertook to make my statistical tables arithmetically correct, a task that deserves and has my gratitude.

Finally, sincere thanks to my secretary, Mrs. Nellie Miedzinski, for her quick and accurate typing of several drafts from copy that was rough indeed.

Frank O'Brien
Washington, November, 1964

Foreword

The economic policy and performance of the Soviet Union is an inescapable part of the environment within which American economic policy must be made. We allocate a large part of our national resources in response to what we believe Soviet intentions and capabilities to be. Beyond this, we have been warned in recent years that we must accelerate our economic growth in order to keep ahead of the Russians, we have been advised to rival or emulate Soviet economic efforts in the developing countries, we have been told that trade with the USSR holds either great opportunities or great dangers for us. Much of this advice was probably mistaken. But our involvement with Soviet economics cannot be denied.

The Committee for Economic Development (CED) has found in much of its past and current work on American economic growth, on policy toward the less developed countries, and on commercial policy, that it had to make judgments about the significance of Soviet economics for us. To inform ourselves better, and to contribute to the better information of others, we commissioned this study by Mr. Frank O'Brien of the CED Research Staff. We asked him to apply his talents as an observer and relater of world affairs to reviewing the available materials, Soviet and Western, and providing an interpretation of them. This is a difficult task, not only because the material is voluminous but also because the value of much of it as evidence is uncertain. In the circumstances, an interpretation can be only that, *an* interpretation, not a final, exclusive judgment. But Mr. O'Brien has performed a valuable service in presenting the evidence and narrowing the range of possible interpretations. We are also pleased that he has not transferred his difficult task to the reader, but has written a readable and exciting book.

9

On behalf of CED I should like to join Mr. O'Brien in his thanks to the people outside CED who provided assistance in this study. I also wish to thank the members of the Editorial Committee, listed elsewhere in this volume, for their cooperation.

Herbert Stein
Director of Research
Committee for Economic Development

Introduction

When work began on this attempt to appraise Soviet domestic and international economic policy in the decade following Stalin's death, the replacement in May, 1960 of Old Bolshevik Kliment Y. Voroshilov by young engineer Leonid I. Brezhnev as President of the USSR offered itself as a starting point. As a press dispatch reporting the event noted, the office involved had always been mainly ceremonial, but the change of occupant was nevertheless a true changing of the guard, the elevation to high office in the Soviet Union of one of the "new men" of Russian Marxism, "weaned on the machine, in industry, agriculture and politics".

The effects upon ideology and economic policy flowing from this changing of the guard throughout Soviet Russia, from the old Bolsheviks who made the 1917 Revolution to the young technologists of post-Revolution Russian Marxism, was one of the intended central interests of the book. So it was that the name of Leonid I. Brezhnev, the man who was eventually to depose Nikita S. Khrushchov and succeed him as First Secretary of the Communist Party of the Soviet Union — the seat of power in the USSR — came to lead all the rest in this report on the Khrushchovian transition years in the evolution of Russian Marxism.

The jettisoning of Khrushchov in the Fall of 1964, as this book was about to go to press, was the outworking of the policies, and of the new ideas, that Khrushchov himself had put into circulation in the Soviet Union; . . . the rough handed dictatorship of the proletariat that carried out the Russian Revolution and carried through the Marxation of Russia should become gentler handed, in order that it should become a more effective, and longer lasting, controlling hand; . . . Russian Marxist policy should become less the thing of personal predilection of a party boss, and more the product of modern committee control, depending for its wisdom less upon personal genius and more upon the more predictable and dependable amalgamation of the expertise of many specialists; . . . effective use of incentives should take the place of the overseer's whip as the chief instrument of economic progress; . . . a socialist nations system, politically and economically integrated under Russian Marxist leadership, should replace the forced subjugation and economic plundering of the satellite states of Eastern Europe; . . . for the most part wars of liberation and violent revolutions should be regarded as having lost much of their usefulness when the colonial system broke up; in short, that order and deftness should replace breakup and brute force as the guiding instruments — internal and international — of Soviet Russia's bid for world supremacy.

What follows here shows, however, that in the latter half of the Khrushchov years Soviet Russia's economic growth was slowing and the attempt to transmute Marxist foreign policy from simple revolutionaryism into a subtle and many faceted use of military, economic, and political forces was tending to end, instead, in a frozen quarrel with Red China, the dilution of Soviet authority among Russia's East European allies, and frustration of Russia's efforts to form one huge integrated whole of the Russian and the East European economies. The slowdown in Russia's economic growth was bringing to an end any hope that Russia could soon produce an affluent communist state or overtake and excel the economic achievements of the United States. All these things taken together tended to dim the Red star that in the 1950s rose as a bright beacon over the free world's underdeveloped and politically undecided lands.

Whether Khrushchov's successors will be able to do better only time can tell. What follows is an examination of their task: Marxism's search for efficiency. It is not Russia's, or Khrushchov's, or Brezhnev's search for efficiency; the task is to find a way to make a *Marxist* society efficient. What follows indicates that the failures, the slowdowns, the frustrations suffered by Russia as it became the world's first mature Marxist state have their roots in Marxism itself. It is these roots that we will be examining.

The examination is aimed at providing the reader with the sort of everyday comprehension of Soviet Russia's economic poli-

12

cies and problems that the non-expert citizen uses in making up his mind about at-home complex questions, such as monetary policy, defense policy, education policy and the like.

It rests fundamentally upon the view that Soviet Russia is in fact engaged in an attempt to gain world primacy by substituting Russian Marxism for competitive self-government and for the competitive, free enterprise economic system.

It seeks to winnow out the elements of USSR economic policy that set Russia apart and help create the Cold War. We know that we cannot deal with Marxist Russia as with other nations. The present book seeks to answer the question, why is that so? This involves questions such as, what are the intractable elements of USSR policy; why is an increase in Russian economic dealings with the underdeveloped countries of the free world regarded in the West as an "economic offensive" rather than a competitive trade drive; why is Russian trade with the United States and other industrialized Western countries subject to special restrictions?

The study focuses upon the Soviet Union because Russia is the focus of the communist world. The other communist nations are treated chiefly as they relate to, influence, and are influenced by the USSR, which is taken as their director in the building of a communist nations system. The growth in the early 1960s of "polycentrism" among Russia's communist allies — several centers, rather than one, of communist authority — reduced Russia's role as boss and placed emphasis and new value upon the development in the Soviet hierarchy of the arts of international leadership, where once the master's voice had sufficed. But by virtue of her greatly superior economic and military weight in the Marxist world, Russia retained a practical and effective first rank in world communism, whatever bows had to be made to sensibilities and national pride elsewhere.

A Statistical Section provides an organized view of the data upon which the study depends. The text avoids, whenever possible, recapitulation of these tables, in favor of non-numerical discussion of the issues the underlying data result from or suggest.

Marxist Russia is viewed as having developed three "Great Claims" as points of attack upon the free world. These are:

1. A claim to be developing, in the USSR, a type of society, founded upon Marxist economic organization, that is better suited to the modern world than is competitive capitalism—a prototype society for the new world now being wrought by scientific and technological change.

2. A claim to be developing, in the nations system of the communist world, a prototype international system of fraternal cooperation and common economic, social and cultural development.

3. A claim to be the guarantor of world peace through the peaceful coexistence policy, of which the Soviet economic offensive in the free world is an adjunct.

In Part I of the study the USSR economy is examined against the backdrop of the First Great Claim, in the form of Russia's assertion that the Soviet Union is near the point of developing the most efficient economy in the world, as the means to the creation of the "most perfect society" of man.

In Part II, the Socialist Nations System is viewed against the Second Great Claim as set forth in the New Program of the Communist Party of the Soviet Union (CPSU), adopted in 1961, wherein it is stated that the CPSU is leading the Marxist nations to "a social, economic, and political community of free sovereign peoples . . . united by common interests and goals . . . governed by laws that ensure rapid, steady and balanced growth of the economies of all the countries belonging to that system. . . ."

Since this is an examination of Soviet economic policy the Third Great Claim is examined, in Part III, chiefly in its Soviet economic policy aspects. These are the consequences in international affairs of USSR trade policy toward, first, the United States and other industrialized countries of the free world, and, second, the underdeveloped countries.

Exception can be taken to the author's view that Soviet official pronouncements, plans, programs, boasts, threats, etc. can and should be taken seriously as indications of Marxist intent. This includes taking exception to serious acceptance of the Soviet claim to be devising the end of capitalism and preparing the world for Russian Marxist ascendancy.

Those who take such exception ask whether it is realistic to argue that the New Program is "anything more than an inspirational statement of the millenial goals of the Communist Party of the Soviet Union," whether the New Program's "rosy-hued future is not just psychic compensation for today's drabness". They take the position that "generalizations about the aim of world domination and 'law governed historical process' tell us little about the real priorities in the minds of the rulers of the USSR". Russia's governing elite is described, in this view, as composed of men caring little if anything for world revolution, being instead intent upon security, power, efficiency and holding what they have on the cold war fronts, Marxists, if at all, only on feast days, when they regale the *hoi polloi* with ritual doctrinal statements.

It is well to have this view in mind as a cautionary reservation, and it is displayed here as such. It is a view that was considered and rejected as a fundamental decision underlying this book. The study *does* pay serious attention, *as indications of intent,* to the statements of Marxist leaders, and to Marxism's central pronouncements, from the Communist Manifesto through the Third Program of the world's reigning Marxist party, the CPSU. The underlying view here *is* that Soviet Russia is quite serious when it states, repeatedly and officially, come political thaw or freeze, that its aim is to destroy the liberal, free enterprise system throughout the world, and to replace it with the authoritarian, Russian Marxist system, ruled and directed by the CPSU. Other communist nations and parties, such as Red China and its Chinese Communist Party, are assumed to have the same aims, but smaller capabilities. Russia's coexistence policy is consequently viewed as an attempt to maintain a hostile, not a peaceful, state of coexistence, with the aim of gradual encroachment and final victory.

This view was chosen because it seemed to the author to be the only reasonable and prudent one. However "practical," "crass," or "security conscious" the high level Soviet official may have become, and even though he is Marxist only on feast days, still, his ambience is Marxism, and he partakes of the essential fears, romanticism and hostility of his system with respect to rival systems. Soviet Russia still does actively pursue, in its concentration of its economic capabilities on military production, its autar-

15

kic attitude to trade, its refusal to cooperate with the West, and its attempts, as in Cuba in 1962, to gain the upper hand by stealth if possible, policies that underwrite its hostile pronouncements. When action thus tends to fit the ideological word, it seems unreasonable and imprudent to take the view that the word, however ritualistic, means something other than what it seems to mean. Therefore, Soviet goals — economic, political, and military — millenial though they may be, are taken here as serious expressions of real intent.

Khrushchov gave expression to the Russian Marxist view of the world that is accepted in this study as giving Soviet policy its basic orientation, in a speech at a meeting dedicated to Soviet-Cuban friendship, in Moscow, May 23, 1963, and reported the following day in the Russian Communist Party newspaper *Pravda*. The Soviet leader said:

> We Marxist-Leninists make no secret of our attempts to draw all people in the world over to the side of socialism. In this we see our most important mission in the world arena. . . . We Marxist-Leninists proceed from the standpoint that peaceful coexistence is the only sensible basis for relations between states having differing social systems. We have always considered this policy handed down to us by Lenin, as the guiding principle of our foreign policy in general. . . . Our party has always held the view that peaceful coexistence creates favorable conditions for promoting the class struggle of the workers in capitalist countries, for furthering the national liberation movement. Experience gained in the people's revolutionary struggle after World War II convincingly demonstrated that it is precisely under conditions of peaceful coexistence, when the socialist countries, together with all peaceloving peoples, restrain the aggressive tendencies of the imperialists, that the worldwide liberation movement gains particular momentum. It was precisely under the conditions of peaceful coexistence with states having different social systems that the glorious Cuban revolution, led by ardent warriors for the cause of the people, was triumphant.

There is no reason to think that Khrushchov's successors have a different view of the aims of Russian coexistence policy.

Nevertheless, much of what follows tends to show that Russia has little or no chance of achieving such goals, provided the United States and others in the free world remain reasonably well united and conduct themselves with reasonable care. That is, *it is also an underlying view* of this book that Russia does not have much practical chance of converting her high flown intentions into fact, now or in the future. But it is assumed that Russia would carry out her I-will-bury-you aims if she could, and that she will at any time go as far toward carrying them out as she can with safety.

It appears to the author that policies resting upon some such view are best calculated to get us forward toward a world of less fear and more international trust. The author believes that policies so derived can wear down, and finally eliminate, Soviet Russia's hostile intent toward us. He believes that such should be *our* intent: to bring Soviet Russia back into the world of nations at peace with one another.

It is the maximum hope of the study that if the elements in Soviet Russia's economic policy that make it hostile and aggressive can be brought out and clarified, a better basis will exist for the development of United States and other free world policy, such as trade policy toward the USSR, that will in time make it possible for Marxist Russia to rejoin the rest of the peaceable world. At the minimum, it is hoped that identification and clarification of the elements in Russian policy that arouse our mistrust would make our defenses easier to maintain, and surer.

The text of the study is expected to be intelligible without reference to the footnotes. The footnotes are of a kind and extent intended to provide readers who want it with additional information, and with a running bibliography, chiefly, the sources used in preparing the study.

A Note on the Government of Soviet Russia

Communist Russia calls itself the Union of Soviet Socialist Republics (USSR). It is a "Soviet" union because in form at least the organization of authority is a pyramid of Soviets — Workers' Councils — proceeding from many local Soviets upwards, through an extensive consolidating system, to the Supreme Soviet of the USSR. The main levels of consolidation are regional, and Republic, Soviets. The regional Soviet is a legislature. The Presidium of the Supreme Soviet is the nation's "permanent" legislature, and the Council of Ministers, headed by the Premier, is the nation's Executive. However, parallel and interlocking formations of the Russian Communist Party — officially called the Communist Party of the Soviet Union (CPSU) — exercise the real control, at all levels from base to pinnacle. The CPSU is fully in command of all Soviets through its ability to select all candidates for election to them by way of a single list of Party-approved candidates.

A report written for the Committee on Government Operations of the US Senate, titled "National Policy Machinery in the Soviet Union," said, with respect to the relationship of Party and Government in the USSR:

"In theory the USSR is a federally organized constitutional democracy. In actuality, however, there exists no concept of the Constitution as a supreme law limiting the powers and operations of government. Despite its democratic trappings, the Soviet Constitution is merely a formal description of the socialist state organization, and thus it chronicles rather than determines the development of the state.

"The membership of the Soviet Communist Party is slightly less than 4 per cent of the total population of the country. This highly disciplined elite exercises firm control and direction of Soviet life through a rigidly hierarchical professional party machine responsive only to the center in Moscow which controls the strategic assignment of Communists to key positions in all institutions and enterprises.

"Party control effectively prevents any genuine exercise of autonomy by governmental bodies.

"At the top of the Soviet administrative structure distinctions of background and function fade. . . . This merging of authority at the top demonstrates the interlocking nature of the Soviet administrative directorate, with parallel lines of party and Government organization extending down through the whole Soviet system. The Soviet Union is a one-party state, ruled by a group of men who exercise effective authority by virtue of their control of the Communist Party."

The Supreme Soviet "elects" the USSR's operating government — the Council of Ministers — approving a list chosen by the

Presidium (formerly Politburo) of the CPSU. The CPSU's Presidium is thus the ruling directorate in the USSR. The leader of the Party Presidium is the First Secretary of the Central Committee of the CPSU. The First Secretary of the CPSU is thus the chief executive of Soviet Russia.

Outline of Part I

I. Marxism in
Search of Efficiency

*"We are perfecting the planning process,
not going away from it."*[1]

**Russian
Marxism**

The papers of May 1, 1960, contained an announcement
that Leonid I. Brezhnev, a metallurgical engineer, had been elected Chairman of the Supreme Soviet of the USSR, replacing an
Old Bolshevik, Marshal Kliment Y. Voroshilov, as titular Chief
of State of the Soviet Union.

One dispatch, seeking for the meaning in this change of faces
in an office almost without authority, noted that Brezhnev "represents a new generation of Soviet figures, men who were born in
this century and are now coming into their own. They were
weaned on the machine, in industry, agriculture and politics."[2]

Despite the strictly ceremonial nature of the chairmanship
of the Supreme Soviet, turning the Old Bolshevik out and putting
the young engineer in his place was significant. It pointed to the
main thing that happened within Soviet Russia in the first decade
after Stalin died: Technological Man clanked up and announced
that he was ready to hatch the Fully Communist Society in Marxist Russia.

---

[1] Modest I. Rubenshtein, Senior Staff Member, Institute of World Economy and International Relations, Moscow, answering a question whether Russia was moving toward
a market economy. The question was asked at a conference on economic growth, in
the New York offices of McGraw Hill, October, 1959, part of a program for a six-man
delegation of Russian economists, of which Rubenshtein was a member, arranged at
government request, by the Committee for Economic Development. Reported by Karl
Schriftgiesser of CED in a memo to CED Trustees, "Story of the Tour" (of the US
by the Russian delegation), March, 1960.

[2] Max Frankel, *New York Times,* May 8, 1960.

21

The point was made more telling by further changes early in the second decade after Stalin. On July 15, 1964 Brezhnev left the presidency and became First Deputy Secretary of the Communist Party of the Soviet Union (CPSU), one step down from Nikita S. Khrushchov,[1] at that time First Secretary of the CPSU and Premier of the Soviet government. Anastas I. Mikoyan, an Old Bolshevik but likewise an old technocrat, assumed the presidency. The shift in Soviet power to the new Marxist breed of Russian "weaned on the machine" was completed on October 14, 1964. Khrushchov was ousted, Brezhnev took over as First Secretary of the CPSU and Aleksei N. Kosygin, a career Marxist planning official, took Khrushchov's place as Premier.

This put Technological Man in full charge of achieving what the Russian Marxist leadership has promised the Russian people — and advised the world — that Marxism will soon accomplish in the first and foremost Marxist state: the creation of a Marxist affluent society, on the basis of which a genuinely communist society could be built (and without which real communism cannot be achieved). As observed in the Introduction, whether the new men can do better than the former leadership had done, only time can tell. *But the New Bolshevik leadership in Russia faces the same root difficulty that the Old Bolshevik leadership faced, and that the Khrushchovian transition leadership could not solve: how to make a Marxist society as efficient and productive as the modern capitalist society.*

This is the problem this book is centrally concerned with: the competition of the Marxist and capitalist systems. We examine here the problems the leadership of Russia must try to solve.

According to Marxist "law" the fully communist society would have to be capable of supplying its people *according to their needs,* not according to the standard used by societies in a "lower stage of development": the standard of how much the individual contributes to production. To operate in this way, the communist society would have to be a high productivity society of people guided in their work and consumption habits by high, socially aware and considerate lights. This morality — Communist Consciousness as it is called — would be engendered in Communist

---

[1] Spelled here more nearly as pronounced than in the usual rendering, Khrushchev.

Man of the fully communist society by the privilege, and tutelage, of living under the guidance of the Communist Party. Communist Man, Communist Consciousness and Communist Society would all be made possible, according to "law governed" processes of Marxism, by the full use of modern technology, under the political supervision of the Communist Party.

In the already highly industrialized West, these great expectations of the machine, and of mankind formed upon it, arouse a jaundiced recollection that we were weaned on the machine — in industry, agriculture and politics — long ago. Mechanization is more likely to bore or repel us than to enchant us. Not that we have not valued the efficiency and plenty the machine has made possible to us. We have made it clear in our civilization that we know what benefits flow from the machine, and that we want to give full scope to mechanization. But we have few expectations of inner enlightenment, or of socially improving benefits, from Technological Man, be he ours or others.

This points to one of our basic difficulties in comprehending and dealing with the USSR: Soviet Russia's enthusiasms are often our commonplaces. There is a reason. Where the stimulus of private profit is lacking something must take its place. The Russians use political pressure. Consequently, we have often observed the USSR bending all efforts in politically fired national campaigns put on to win what we had already long taken for granted. This has made for underestimation of the USSR. It appears that the Russians have often underestimated *our* strength, and misinterpreted *our* intentions for the reverse reason: because we do not bother to make show over matters that are important, but familiar, to us. We make few speeches about our cultural efficiency, our fine communications and transportation, our sophisticated technology, the fruitfulness of human effort when capitalized as only we capitalize it. We are more likely to make critical speeches in these areas. It is hard for the Russians to understand that this is the competitive, private enterprise way of getting further progress.

There is an added and related difficulty affecting our ability to place a proper estimate upon the state and meaning of things in communist Russia: the time element. Communist leaders have habitually held their celebrations before the victory, claiming for the present or the near future advances not yet made, advances that would come about, if at all, only in a fairly distant future, and perhaps in smaller measure than claimed. This has often led us to believe that life in communist Russia is chiefly a huge fantasy. The result was that we have been excessively surprised and impressed by proof of real achievements, as when Sputnik I flew. Earlier, we had been taken aback when Russia turned up in the middle of the 1950s offering economic help to the underdeveloped countries of the free world. These were developments that *should* have followed upon large scale industrialization such as Russia has undergone, and they would not have been surprising except that our view of the USSR had been unrealistically low.

In Part I we will try to sort reality from the yet-if-ever-to-be with respect to the USSR's First Great Claim: that the USSR stands upon the verge of the here-now creation of a Marxist affluent society in which can be produced a superior human creature, Communist Man, capable of leading the rest of the world to social justice and economic plenty under Marxism.

Whatever the worth of this Great Claim, at the least a Great Reality is involved. *Unless the USSR can produce an affluent society from its way of communist life at home, there is little chance of making Russian Marxism a world way of life.* And, as Communist China has had to learn, the leaders of Soviet Russia are not interested just in leading the world to Marxism; they are intent upon leading a world *Russian* Marxist movement. Consequently, success in making Russian communism yield the first and best Marxist Good Life is critical to Russia's communist leadership.

The situation of the Russian economy is therefore our starting place. We will approach by way of a birdseye view from the outside, as an introductory perspective.

Since the Marxist Revolution in Russia in 1917, Russia has risen from last and least of the Western Great Powers to be the second. Her economy is now second in size only to that of the US. But, if we look at Column 3 of Table 1,[1] we see that the USSR economy produces only about two-thirds as much per man, woman and child (that is, per capita) as do the economies of

---

[1] Tables 1 to 20 are in the Statistical Section, between Part I and Part II.

France, Germany and the UK. The USSR economy produces only about 40 per cent as much, per capita, as does the US economy. Column 7 of Table 1 shows what is left for private consumption after production used for investment, defense and other government purposes is taken out. This shows that per capita *consumption* (as distinguished from per capita production) in Italy is a good deal larger than per capita consumption in Russia. Such a comparison demonstrates the cost, in standard of living, of intense concentration on production for industrial expansion and military output. Heavy concentration on the industry-military complex has been Marxism's unchanging policy in Russia, and the same priorities remain in Russia's plans through 1980.[1]

Russia has rebounded stronger than before from truly appalling losses of human life and material wealth in World War II. She has learned to use her inadequate economic capacity selectively, to achieve something like military and scientific parity with the United States. She has mastered and put into use the general body of Western industrial technology (but her industrial technology and productivity are low by American standards and

---

[1] A Note on Measuring the Economy of the Soviet Union:

The calculations of the experts who prepared the studies *Dimensions of Soviet Economic Power* (1962) and *Annual Economic Indicators for the U.S.S.R.* (1964) for the Joint Economic Committee of the Congress are used in this study as the basis for discussion of Soviet economic trends and comparison of Soviet and US and other free world economies. Extensive discussions of methodology were given in each of the Joint Economic Committee reports mentioned (pages 69-89 in *Dimensions* and pages 91-98 in *Annual Economic Indicators*). The 1964 study reflects the conviction among Western students of the USSR economy that the Soviet Union's growth rate declined sharply after 1958, due mainly to unfavorable manpower conditions and to disastrous agricultural failures, the latter in part due to bad weather. However, even eliminating the effects of weather, there would have been a substantial decline in the USSR economic growth rate after 1958 (to something like 5 percent in 1963), *Annual Indicators* suggests.

Some students of the Soviet economy have long believed that even the USSR growth rates generally accepted in the West for the early and middle 1950s were too high, although they were much lower than Soviet claims. See the *Note on Industrial Indexes,* following Table 5.

The estimates worked out with considerable care in *Dimensions* and in *Annual Indicators* are accepted here as being as reliable as possible given the lack of complete data. They take account of major objections raised against the basic data and the estimates they use. They are therefore to a significant degree new and independent estimates. They are, nevertheless, still estimates, depending to a considerable extent upon judgments made by individuals, but they are careful estimates, intended to come as close as possible to reality. Those wishing to know how the estimates were made, the data upon which they rest, and the main judgments exercised in making them should consult the pages noted above in *Dimensions* and *Annual Indicators*.

A discussion of the causes of the Soviet economic downturn will be found in "Going Fast More Slowly: Industry", in Section I of this Study.

25

her agriculture is backward). Communist Russia has put on a pyrotechnic display of industrial growth. But her agricultural output has grown little with respect to population.

Meanwhile, the USSR has helped into being a socialist nations system with a third of the world's three billion population. (Table 7 gives a statistical profile of the communist world.) In the 1950s, the USSR reached out, economically and politically, into the underdeveloped part of the free world, where live very nearly half the world's people. In a very short time Russia made herself at home among many of the underdeveloped free world countries as an economic and political instructor, representing her Marxist way to be the best and quickest way of national improvement.

Perhaps the most important accomplishment of Soviet Russia is an at-home triumph: there is evidence that the communist government and system has won the consent of the majority of the people of the USSR.[1] Without this triumph, Marxist Russia would be fatally weak; given it, Marxist Russia is a world power.

Table 1 compares the chief characteristics of the USSR economy, after nearly half a century of Marxism, with the same characteristics of the world's other principal industrial countries.

The following observations seem in order:

1. After nearly half a century of Marxism:

   a) (Cols. 4, 5 & 6) Russia's rate of economic growth is very high, but two capitalist countries—West Germany and Japan—that were also recovering from great war losses and were, like the USSR, intent on economic expansion, had comparable or higher rates of economic growth, throughout the 1950's and early 1960's. Italy's growth rate was very close to Russia's. It should be noted that West Germany, Japan and Italy carried only small defense burdens, while Russia's was comparable to ours. The same observations, applying to the same countries, hold for increases in economic efficiency (Cols. 16 & 17).

   b) (Cols. 9-11) Soviet Russia achieves a very high rate of capital investment, but so also do two nations—West Germany and Japan —depending on market forces, not governmental direction, to mobilize savings.

2. (Col. 2) The USSR has become a big economy. Nevertheless, the economic capacity available to it is not quite half as large as ours.

---

[1] For a collection of evidence on this point, see *The Soviet Citizen*, by Alex Inkeles and R. A. Bauer, Harvard University Press, Cambridge, Mass., 1959.

To have become a respected competitor of the United States in basic industry, science, space propulsion and conventional and nuclear military capability, with only half the economic force, shows ability to select and pursue goals, despite handicaps, that we should not forget.

3. (Cols. 7-15) This competitive parity with the United States in the matters that are of the highest priority to Russia's communist leadership has been taken out of the living standard of the Russian people, by withholding much of what they produce from them in favor of investment and defense.

4. (Cols. 4, 5, & 6) Russia's economic elan was much greater than that of the United States and Great Britain, the first and the third ranking free world economies, from 1950-58. But Russia's economic dash is slowing down. In 1960-63 US growth was probably the higher, and Russia's was only a little better than half what it was in 1950-58.

5. (Cols. 10, 11, 16 & 17) Marxism has not altered the basic economic proportions as they are known to capitalism. The USSR's annual average investment as a per cent of her total economic activity, although very high, is within the range of investment in capitalist countries. Higher rates of investment are needed in Marxist Russia, as elsewhere, to produce extraordinary increases in productivity and economic growth.

6. Sheer size, and sheer qualitative lead, are dynamic factors with their own meaning. The United States economy is over twice the size of the USSR economy. This fact, associated with two others not in Table 1, make communist Russia's goal of overtaking and surpassing the United States an economically overwhelming task. The other two facts are that Russia's industrial efficiency is less than half that of the US, and her agricultural efficiency is less than a quarter of ours.[1] The *size* of these US leads is so great that *very* much higher growth rates, maintained over *very* long times, are needed to overcome them.

Communist Russia has progressed since 1917 from an immature to a mature economy, from an immature to a mature polity, and from isolation as a single pariah Marxist state to the leadership of a Marxist Nations System, controlling a third of humanity. What follows here most often stresses the economic problems that Soviet Russia faces. This does not imply that Russia has nothing but problems. It is on the theory that problems, not

---

[1] As used here, economic efficiency is intended to mean what economists mean by labor productivity — that is, the amount of output per input in the economy, or some sector of it.

accomplishments, are the seed of policy, and it is a perspective on policy we are after. At any rate, but for a great degree of success, Russia would have few problems that would concern *us*.

Russia's economic (and social, etc.) problems are the problems of becoming mature. For Russia, the problems of maturing are unique, because no other society has reached Russia's condition of internal development and external power and responsibility under Marxist guidance. It is these problems of the newly adult Marxist nation and newly arrived Marxist world power that the "Soviet new man" has come on to solve — and to establish and strengthen Soviet Russia in the process. His idol is the machine. His middle name is Technology. His scripture is the State Plan. He is in search of a higher order of efficiency, by which to make the industrialized, matured Russian communist state the best achievement of the 20th Century, and the mold for the 21st Century.

This would be a way of life as remote from the rude, cruel, knocked-together communism of the first few decades of Russian Marxism as current liberalistic, publicly supervised and conditioned capitalism is remote from the callow *laissez faire* capitalism of the 18th Century.[1] This does not imply a liberalistic Soviet society in the future. It only implies a more sophisticated, better

---

[1] Many, perhaps most, experts on the communist countries would prefer a more specialized use of the term Marxism to the usage here. Their view is probably represented by the following comment from Dr. Gregory Grossman, of the University of California, at Berkeley:

"No one would deny that Marxism had *something* to do with the Bolshevik revolution and subsequent events in that part of the world, but just how much and in what ways Marxism can explain these events is subject to lively debate among specialists, and will continue to be. Certainly, Marxism cannot explain everything about the Soviets and other communists and their countries. And besides, there was more than one kind of Marxism in 1903, 1917, 1924 (to pick a few crucial dates in the history of Bolshevism), let alone 1963."

This view is certainly no less correct than would be a similar criticism of the use of the word capitalist to describe and explain the origins and policies of the United States, Great Britain, France, Japan, etc., in their modern forms. Marxism is used here in about the way we use the term capitalism, except that there is no one written source for the philosophy of capitalism. It would be difficult to find another term (communism, bolshevism, socialism, etc.) that would be more accurate than Marxism as a shorthand reference to the political structures, the works and the policies claiming, at least, to grow from the work of Karl Marx and Friedrich Engels.

The author feels better about persisting in his unspecialized use of the term Marxism by having Professor Grossman's critique to display as a corrective. Perhaps it should be added that someone has said that ideas are not responsible for their interpreters.

calculated, better satisfied Marxist society. That could well turn out to be a more effectively controlled society than today's, albeit more discreetly controlled.

Overtake and Excel
Capitalism

This qualitative triumph is expected to follow upon a great quantitative achievement: catching up with and excelling capitalism's mightiest work, the economy of the United States.

Just before the USSR launched its current (1959-65) Seven Year Plan of economic development, N. S. Khrushchov, then Soviet Premier and First Secretary of the Communist Party of the Soviet Union[1], told a gathering of graduates of USSR military academies:

> The superiority of the USSR in the speed of growth of production will create a real basis for insuring that within a period of, say, five years following 1965, the level of US production per capita should be equalled and overtaken. Thus, by that time, perhaps even sooner, the USSR will have captured first place in the world both in absolute volume of production and per capita production, which will ensure the world's highest standard of living.[2]

---

[1] The following is a thumbnail chronology of USSR leadership from Stalin through October 1964: Nikita S. Khrushchov became First Secretary of CPSU on Sept. 7, 1953, six months after Georgi Malenkov assumed Party and governmental control in Russia following Joseph Stalin's death on March 5, 1953. Malenkov remained Chairman of the government until Feb. 8, 1955, when Nikolai A. Bulganin took over. Bulganin and Khrushchov shared power in Russia until March 31, 1958, when Khrushchov formally completed his advance to sole dominance by taking over the office of Premier. Leonid I. Brezhnev took Krushchov's place as First Secretary, and Aleksei N. Kosygin his place as Premier, on Oct. 14, 1964. For a full chronology of the main events in USSR history in the first decade following Stalin's death, see *Problems of Communism*, Vol. XII, No. 2, (United States Information Agency, Washington 25, D.C.), March-April, 1963.

[2] Quoted in *Soviet World Outlook*, Department of State Publication 6836.

Bibliographical Note: Problems of Communism is a quarterly published by the United States Information Agency, Washington, D.C. It is available at 35¢ per copy, or $1.50 per year, from the US Government Printing Office, Washington 25, D.C., or, *gratis* from any United States Information Office outside the United States. It is one of several periodicals dealing with the communist world which were principal sources for this study. Two others, both published by Ilford House, London and both available in this country through Eastern News Distributors, Inc., 255 Seventh Ave., New York City, are *Survey* (formerly *Soviet Survey*), published six times yearly, $3 per year, and *China Quarterly*, $4 per year. Another is *Studies on the Soviet Union*, published by The Institute for the Study of the USSR, Munich, four times yearly, $6.

In 1961, with the Seven Year Plan in full swing, the CPSU issued its Third Program,[1] generally called the New Program. The long-term Third Program reiterated the goal Khrushchov had set in 1958, again giving 1970 as the year for overtaking the US. It spelled out what such an achievement would mean in the lives of the people of Russia, in phrases with a familiar utopian ring.

> In the current decade (1961-1970) the Soviet Union, in creating the material and technological basis of communism, will surpass the strongest and richest capitalist country, the USA, in production per head of population, the people's standard of living and their cultural and technical standards will improve substantially, everyone will live in easy circumstances, all collective and state farms will become highly productive and profitable enterprises, the demand of the Soviet people for well-appointed housing will, in the main, be satisfied, hard, physical work will disappear, the USSR will become the country with the shortest working day.[2]

It takes only a little arithmetic to show that in fact the USSR has no chance to overtake the US in per capita production by the end of the current decade. Table 2 shows the basic data and the arithmetic.

Using economic growth and population growth rates that are the most favorable to Russia, in 1970 the Russian people will produce only $1,997 per man, woman and child, or *some $1,000 less per person than was already produced in the United States in 1962.* If we follow the Soviet Russian economic growth curve on its downward path since 1958[3], we get the following less opti-

---

[1] The First Program of the Bolshevik Party (which became the CPSU) was adopted in 1903. It called for the overthrow of the Czarist regime and the seizure by the state of all property in Russia, plus the installation of a dictatorship of the proletariat, to lead the nation toward communism. The Second Program was adopted in 1919, upon the full realization of the First Program. The Second Program was a plan for building a socialist society in Russia as the precondition to communism. The Third Program, adopted in 1961, declared that this second stage of Marxist work in Russia had also been accomplished, and that the nation was now ready to build the fully communist society. It laid down a long-term outline of a plan for building the world's first true communist society as the final and complete work of Marxism in Russia. The very important, in fact crucial, dynamics of the differences in the Russian Marxist view between the capitalist and socialist, and the socialist and communist societies will be discussed later.

[2] This, and other quotations from the Third Program, are taken from the English language version of the draft text of the Program published in *The New York Times* of August 1, 1961. The draft text was adopted by the Twenty Second Congress of the CPSU, held in October, 1961.

[3] See Table 1 for growth rates.

mistic results for USSR per capita output in 1970:

$1,618, projecting the 1958-62 growth rate.
$1,454, projecting the 1960-63 estimated rate.

The United States economy will meanwhile be growing. The higher of two rates of population increase for the United States used in the *Statistical Abstract*[1] for 1963 indicated a possible average annual population growth of 1.7 per cent for 1960-70. The average annual US economic growth rate 1950-60 was 3.3 per cent (Table 1). If these rates are projected from 1962, when US per capita output was $3,004 (Table 2) to 1970, US production per person in 1970 would come to some $3,410. This is nearly 70 per cent higher than the highest projection of Soviet per capita output in 1970, and much more than double two less optimistic expectations for the Soviet Union in 1970, given just above.

If the Russian consumer continues to get for his personal use some two-fifths of the nation's output, and the US consumer continues to get about three-fifths, as in 1962 (Table 1), per capita *consumption* in the two countries in 1970 will be about as follows:

USSR: $837 (if per capita GNP were $1,997 (+ 72% over 1962)
$678 (if per capita GNP were $1,618 (+ 40%)
$609 (if per capita GNP were $1,454 (+ 25%)

US: $2,141 (if per capita GNP were $3,410 (+ 13%)

The above are not refined calculations. But they suggest what is within the realm of reasonable expectation. They indicate not only that the Soviet living standard cannot rise above ours by 1970 (or for a very long time after) but also that by the end of this decade Russia will definitely not be producing enough for everyone to live, in the language of the Third Program, "in easy circumstances".

Somewhat unexpected support for this view, from leading USSR economists, was disclosed late in 1963 by the *New York Times'* specialist on the Soviet economy:

---

[1] Department of Commerce, *Statistical Abstract of the United States,* 1963.

In contrast to Premier Khrushchov's usual ebullient predictions about the rapidity with which the Soviet economy is said to be catching up with that of the United States, senior Soviet economists appear to have been emphasizing the difficulties involved and discouraging excessive optimism.

Warnings began to appear several months ago in the Soviet press against accepting an American estimate that Soviet industrial output in 1960 was 75 per cent of the United States figure.

Another recent article by a Soviet economist, V. Sobel, warned his colleagues that (due to differences in statistical handling of amortization in the US and the USSR) United States national income is even higher above the Soviet Union's than the adjusted figures would indicate.

But perhaps the most potent blow in the campaign against Soviet over-optimism has been struck by the dean of Soviet economists, Stanislav G. Strumilin . . . Professor Strumilin's estimates indicate that in the last three years the Soviet Union has made almost no progress in catching up with the United States in total production. According to his calculations, Soviet national income in 1960 was 61.8 per cent of the American level, 62.7 per cent in 1961 and 62.8 per cent in 1962.

At the rate of gain indicated by Professor Strumilin for 1960-62, the Soviet Union would not catch up with the United States until after the year 2000, rather than by 1970 as Premier Khrushchov has maintained. Professor Strumilin's calculations are controversial because he bases his estimates on a method that finds the cost of a particular ration of foods for consumers in both countries, then expresses the national incomes of the two countries in terms of these rations.

While this method is by no means accepted by all economists, the interesting point seems to be . . . that Professor Strumilin dared publish the results of (his) computations.[1]

Why, then, was so impossible a goal chosen and publicized in the Soviet Union? There are probably two main reasons:

First, the simple reason that striving after a higher goal will probably get one farther than striving after a lower goal.

Second, miscalculation in the Russian leadership as to the real Soviet economic growth rate (especially as to agriculture), plus the unquenchable Marxist faith that capitalism is on the verge of collapse while the Marxist society has special wellsprings of dynamism that will permit it to achieve miracles.

Nevertheless, we cannot afford to relax and ignore our communist competition for the world's favor:

---

[1] Harry Schwartz, *New York Times,* September 15, 1963.

1. The hard run the Russians are making at us is forcing their — Marxist — system to perform near the top of its bent. If we should relax, and perform well below the top of our — free enterprise — bent, with high unemployment, low growth rates, low innovation, and gathering obsolescence, our system, while still far ahead at the end of the decade, would nevertheless give off a decaying air, while the communist system, although still far behind in every measurable way, could present itself to an undecided world as the youth of the future.

2. If we look behind the important present fact of the long United States lead over the USSR in per capita GNP (and the large leads held by West Germany, the United Kingdom and France), a somewhat different picture appears.

The large — prospective — fact on the Russian side is that per capita consumable GNP will probably increase somewhere between a fifth and three-fifths by 1970, most likely around a third (see the calculations above). Viewed from inside Russia, this is a prospect for a very great gain, in a very short time. A rise of a third in the amount of goods and services available to improve upon what has for nearly half a century been a dull and deprived daily life would be a joyous event. It would probably leave most Russians little concerned whether Russia had surpassed the United States.

If events should permit a significant reduction of military outlays during the 1960-70 decade, bigger gains in the Soviet living standard could be made.

A sizeable increase in the resources available for improving the quality of life in the USSR would make available to the USSR government large amounts of goods and services for selective use in improving Soviet Russia's world image. This could be done by concentrating on dressing up life in the major cities, and by some other selective major improvements, such as much better clothing, widespread TV coverage and reception, improvement of the quality of the Russian diet (by making such things as tropical fruits commonly available), and, above all, by giving the Russian a lot more of what he has lacked most of all: housing space.

The effect upon a world contemplating the relative benefits

of capitalism and Marxism will depend to a considerable extent upon what we are doing, meanwhile, with our increasing wealth. The size of the economic resources available to us is so great that we could make improvements in the quality of American capitalistic life that no Marxist society could touch. We could altogether eliminate involuntary poverty. We could use automation to make really huge gains in our productivity. We could use the resultant increase in our per capita output to begin creating a new and exciting way of life under free enterprise. This would include such costly things as much better education for all, much better health care, much greater knowledge of and use of the cultural treasures of civilization, and much more travel and participation in the arts.

Simulate the Capitalist Market

The Third Program reveals, in the passage quoted a few pages back, and in many other passages, that Marxism's technological "new" man hides beneath his clanking exterior a romantic faith that Marxism, in and of itself, can somehow make men better. The Third Program, like the First and the Second, displays a messianic faith that if only everyone would embrace the Marxist organization of society without reserve, personal cupidity, evil, etc., would be swept away. Men would be raised to a new plane on which they would do good for the sake of doing good rather than for personal benefit. Socialist society would run itself, guided to what is right by "communist consciousness".

Communist consciousness would be able without fail to distinguish the good from the meretricious, and would be able without room for argument to sort the real needs of society and of the individual from mere whims or selfish desires.

Such Marxist romanticism is probably the chief handicap of the communist society trying to excel capitalism. It befogs the Marxist's appraisal of the effectiveness of the free, competitive 20th Century market in allocating economic resources for efficient use without resort to economic cruelty. It camouflages the crucial fact that capitalism has learned that most reforms can be made to serve the interests of all, including the interest of those being reformed. It makes it difficult for the Marxist to see how capitalism has learned to keep men hard at work for their personal benefit while making personal benefit work for the general welfare. In general, the Marxist has trouble seeing beyond the glare of his political faith to the fact that although capitalism does not work perfectly, it works well, and that it both permits and promises indefinite further refinement and improvement.

But we should not be misled by the New Program's romantics into thinking — again — that Russian Marxist life is a fantasy. The real-world responsibilities of actual government has forced increasing realism upon Russia's Marxist leaders.

Finding a Way for Communism to Live with Marxism

We take up here one of the most troublesome aspects of real-life communist government. The Polish philosopher of communism, Oskar Lange, described the problem in 1958, writing for the Polish Institute of International Affairs.[1] Lange said:

Marx "paid very little attention, as have his followers since, to the problems of economic optimum", because Marx was concerned with "political economy" rather than with "economics". That is, Lange explained, Marx's interest was not in the most efficient ways to *produce* goods and services. Marx was interested in the political organization that can be built upon the "science" of how the products of an economy are *distributed*.

Lange had much earlier (in the 1930s) offered a solution to the difficulties created by this separation of Marxism from operative reality. This was "market socialism", socialism in which Marxist government would (1) permit the price system rather than Party directed planners, to do the work of equating supply and demand, (2) instruct the managers of the state owned production system to manage their enterprises so as to make the maximum profit, under prices that equate supply and demand.

---

[1] Quoted by Alec Nove, in *Communist Economic Strategy: Soviet Growth and Capabilities,* National Planning Association, Washington, D.C., 1959, p. 31.

Market socialism relieves the Marxist government using it of the drudgery and responsibility of fixing every price, and of planning every detail of production. But the state remains the owner of the means of production and the state continues to plan the overall goals of economic development. Since prices are free to respond to competitive market forces *only within* the framework of the state's Marxist goals, and since profits go to the state, effective direction of economic development remains with the government. *What is shocking to Marxism in market socialism is this: part of the Communist Party's complete, sole and final authority over every activity is sacrificed. This happens because an autonomous force — competition for the use of economic resources with prices, not the Party, as the referee — is permitted to determine how much of what gets produced when,* within general directions established by the Plan.

Yugoslavia has put into practice a system very much like Lange's market socialism.[1] Khrushchov exhibited interest in the Yugoslav version of market socialism when he paid a visit to Yugoslav dictator Tito in the summer of 1963. Khrushchov had, of course, been familiar with Lange's proposals for decades, and he had often denounced Yugoslavia's "Workers' Councils" as a capitalistic deviation from Marxism. But in 1963 he said, while in Yugoslavia, that the USSR was planning to "democratize" its economic management and that Russia would "investigate" the Workers' Councils system of management.[2]

This was a remarkable statement, even if chiefly propagandistic. It permitted the idea to get out that the need for reform to achieve greater efficiency had become so acute in the leading Marxist state that the Soviet leadership was actually prepared to think about what had been the unthinkable: depriving the Communist Party of an important part of its complete authority over all things in Soviet Russia. Such would be the effect of substituting an autonomous force, the workings of supply and demand as

---

[1] An English language description of the Yugoslav "Workers' Council" system of approximate market socialism can be found in *Economic Bulletin for Europe,* Vol. 10, No. 3, 1958, "Economic Planning and Management in Yugoslavia" (United Nations Economic Commission for Europe, Sales Section, UN, New York). See also, Brezezinski, *The Soviet Bloc, Unity and Conflict* (Harvard University Press, Cambridge, Mass., 1960), Chapter 9.

[2] *New York Times,* August 21, 1963.

signalled by the price system, in the place of complete, Party controlled planning.[1]

It was clear that the leading communist state was still searching, after nearly half a century in power, for a way to accommodate the necessities of real-life communist administration to the Marxist scripture.

The State
of the Leading Communist
Nation's Economy

As one seeks to reconstruct a picture of the Soviet economy in those late winter days of 1953 when the dictator (Stalin) lay dying, the epithets "grim", or "oppressive" and "bleak" haunt the mind. True, the repair of the enormous wartime physical damage had been nearly completed. Industrial production had been rising rapidly since the end of the war, and even the output of manufactured consumers goods was already considerably above the 1940 level . . .

But grim, oppressive and bleak the economic picture still was. . . . The economy continued mobilized on a quasi-military footing to speed reconstruction, to conduct the cold war, to master atomic weaponry and rocketry, and to support the war in Korea. . . . The "cult of the personality", that is, Stalin's unbridled and capricious despotism, was felt by everyone and everything. Millions of persons were leading a semi-

---

[1] Since the USSR has become so identified with unlimited, centrally directed, national economic planning, and since all-out planning has become the hallmark of any Marxist economy, it is interesting to note that at the outset of Marxist control in the USSR central, national planning (as distinguished from local, or single-industry, planning) was not accepted, and that a proposal to go to central planning, by Trotsky, was seized upon by Stalin as a deviationist idea which Stalin could, and did, use as a principal weapon to beat Trotsky out of the Party and out of the country. But first there were five years of bitter debate of the subject. Soon after Stalin broke Trotsky as his chief rival for power, Stalin instituted central planning in the USSR. The first Five Year Plan began in 1928. See the British historian, Edward H. Carr, in *Socialism in One Country*, 1924-26, Macmillan Company, New York, 1958, p. 498 *et seq.*, where he says:

"The spring of 1924 was marked by a cautious advance in the (CPSU) toward the acceptance of the principle and practice of planning. The prospects of planning after Lenin's final collapse in the spring of 1923 seemed by no means reassuring. The loudly advertised association of Trotsky . . . with the demand for more planning made it impossible for the triumvirate (ruling for Lenin) to espouse the cause. . . . The condemnation of Trotsky and of the opposition at the thirteenth party conference of January, 1924 was unexpectedly followed by a series of measures which for the first time gave planning a central place in economic policy." What had existed previously, Carr says, was "mainly . . . the drawing up of plans for particular industries." (Quoted by permission of the Macmillan Company.)

human existence in forced labor camps . . . real wages were still considerably below the level prevailing before the Five Year Plan began (1928), the peasants' incomes very much lower. . . . Urban housing was a particularly dismal element, with living space per person, though more ample than in 1940, still one fifth below what it was in 1926. The output of the (agricultural) sector was barely above the 1928 level . . . and even in 1928 the Russian diet was one of the poorest in Europe. . . . The other sectors of the economy also had their woes . . . overcentralization and overbureaucratization; cumbersome and often inept planning, which paid virtually no attention to economic efficiency, technological conservatism . . . an elaborate incentive structure in part ineffective and in part perversely effective; a bad price structure . . . emphasis upon quantity of output at the expense of quality, chronic shortages of industrial supplies and equipment . . .[1]

These were only the principal items in Stalin's bequest to his successors in March, 1963. In a book-length study of what life in Soviet Russia was like as Stalin neared his end, Alex Inkeles and R. A. Bauer of the Harvard Russian Research Center suggest[2] that by the time Stalin died, the Russian had been harried, harrassed, terrorized, and propagandized beyond the point of additional returns to the speed of Russian economic development. Discontent may have been rising toward actual breakdown. That is, the post-Stalin technological "new class" came along in Russia just in time with a change of method. From 1953 through most of 1958, Stalin's successors put their more sophisticated methods to work in a rescue operation that gave the Soviet economy a new stimulus and a new period of high economic growth. But after 1958, despite the new methods, there was a renewal of the slowdown that had crept over the Russian economy in the final years of Stalin's life.

Improvement and Relapse: Agriculture

Stalin's successors were agreed that agriculture was their most pressing economic problem. In fact, agricultural failure had become, and remains, characteristic of Marxist government every-

---

[1] Gregory Grossman, "The Soviet Economy," in *Problems of Communism,* Vol. XII, No. 2, April, 1963.

[2] *The Soviet Citizen,* previously cited, especially "Part Three: The Individual and the State".

where. It would be a signal triumph for Russia to overcome her agricultural deficiencies, because the lag in agricultural per capita output has assumed the possible proportions, in the Marxist world, of a general limiting factor to economic progress as a whole. This is so vital a problem that it is worth a small exploration of its general aspect, together with a look at Russia's particular agricultural problems, and her efforts to solve them.[1]

Stalin's successors have not been so profligate in anything as in schemes for reorganizing agriculture in the USSR. They have tried nearly everything but what works in capitalistic countries: make it possible for the worker in agriculture to profit according to the energy and ingenuity he puts into his work, and, let agriculture have its fair share of investment.

That giving the peasant a chance to profit in accordance with his labors and his skills would do wonders in Russia also is illustrated by a single astonishing fact about Soviet agriculture:

Side-by-side with the large scale socialized agriculture of collective and state farms is a private sector of small garden plots — averaging approximately two-thirds of an acre — which the regime permits members of collective farms, employees of state farms, and certain other members of the citizenry to maintain.

Although these plots constituted only 1.4 per cent of the total agricultural land area, and 3.3 per cent of total sown area in 1962, they accounted for about a third of gross agricultural output — including almost half of the total output of livestock products.[2]

---

[1] For a more complete analysis of Soviet agriculture than can be attempted here see: Lazar Volin in *Problems of Communism,* Vol. VIII, No. 1; *Dimensions of Soviet Economic Power,* Part II; *Annual Economic Indicators for the U.S.S.R.,* Section II; *Studies on the Soviet Union,* Vol. II, Nos. 1 and 3; *Problems of Communism,* Vol. XII, Nos. 2 and 3; *Survey,* Nos. 47 and 48; L. W. Witt, "Potentials of New Markets for Agricultural Products", in *Farming, Farmers and Markets for Farm Goods,* a Supplementary Paper of the Committee for Economic Development (1962); United Nations, *Economic Bulletin for Europe,* Vol. 14, No. 2; Theodore W. Schultz, *Transforming Traditional Agriculture,* Yale University Press (1964); and U.S. Department of Agriculture, *Soviet Agriculture Today* (1963).

[2] *Soviet Agriculture Today,* p. 11, (emphasis added). This section on USSR agriculture uses the USDA document extensively. *Soviet Agriculture Today* reported the findings of an official delegation from the US to the USSR for the purpose of examining Soviet agriculture. The delegation was led by Secretary O. L. Freeman and included six top USDA agronomists and agricultural economists.

That is, the peasant when working for himself, produces nearly a third of all USSR farm output on only a thirtieth of the nation's sown land. This is the same peasant who produces so little as a collective farmer or state farm employee. The private plots he makes so productive are bits of the collectives and state farms.

The record of the collective and state farms is dismal:

> With approximately 54 per cent of the total sown area (in the USSR) and 45 per cent of total animal units, collective farms produced approximately 44 per cent of total agricultural output in 1962 according to official Soviet statistics.[1]
> Although state farms accounted for approximately 43 per cent of the total sown area and 27 per cent of total animal units in 1962 they produced only one quarter of the total agricultural output, according to official Soviet statistics. Many of the state farms are in semi-arid regions of low and unstable yields.[1]

In theory, a collective farm is a producer cooperative, managed by a "democratically elected" chairman and board of directors. In practice, supervision and control by the CPSU and the government are stringent, extending to the selection of managerial personnel and to nearly all operational details.

Collectives differ from state farms in two main respects: (1) members of collectives do not receive a wage, but are paid out of the earnings of their particular collective, of which they are shareholders, and (2) the government does not finance investment in the collectives — investment funds come out of the earnings of the collective.

> In Stalin's words, the "first commandment" of the collective farm is the delivery of agricultural products to the state. After fulfilling its obligation to sell stipulated quantities at fixed prices to the state, and of providing for its seed and feed requirements, any remaining production can be sold on private markets. From the total income received, production expenses must be met and approximately one quarter to one third of the monetary income is set aside for investment. The remainder of the income is used to compensate members of the farm for their participa-

---

[1]*Soviet Agriculture Today,* pp. 10 and 11.

tion in the work. . . . Payments to the workers vary with the skill required and the amount of labor accomplished. The payments are determined by a cumbersome procedure, resembling a piece-rate system.[1]

By Soviet definition, the state farm is a "highly mechanized state agricultural enterprise. All work is subordinated to the interest of the socialist state and is conducted strictly on the basis of the national plan". This puts the state farm in the same category as factories and retail shops, or any other earning property of the government. Their profits go to the governmental treasury. Their losses are made up out of the treasury's funds. The government is responsible for investment. Workers on state farms are wage employees of the nation.

The tables on the following page give a picture of the make-up and productivity of USSR agriculture. (See Table 3 in the Statistical Section for a general comparison of the main features of US and USSR agriculture.)

What stands out is the superb productivity of US private enterprise agriculture by comparison with the production of farm goods in Soviet Russia.

Theodore W. Schultz, an American authority in the economics of agriculture, has tried to identify the problems involved in transforming low-yield agriculture into high-productivity agriculture. He concludes that Marxist countries have been outstandingly unsuccessful in improving their agriculture. Schultz assigns lack of proper personal incentive an important place among the causes of this failure. He singles out several other reasons, some of them underlying the failure to provide the farmer with personal incentive.

Together, his reasons for the persistent backwardness of agriculture in Marxist countries add up to an answer to the question: What is it *about Marxist administration of an economy* that leads to agricultural stagnation?

---

[1] *Soviet Agriculture Today,* p. 7. (Anyone wanting an amusing and intimate picture of the almost unbelievable lack of enterprise, and general slacking, that the collective farm system endures can find it in a Soviet novel, *The New Life, A Day on a Collective Farm,* by Fyodor Abramov, first published in January, 1963 in the Leningrad literary monthly *Neva,* of which Abramov is an editor. Available in the United States in a Grove Press paperback, as a Black Cat Book, titled as above).

Farming in the USSR

1. ORGANIZATION AND OUTPUT, 1962	STATE FARMS[1]	COLLEC- TIVES	SOCIALIZED FARMING UNITS	PRIVATE PLOTS
Number of USSR farms	8,600	40,600	49,200	25,800,000
	— Per cent of Total —			
Sown area	49.5%	49.1%	98.6%	1.4%
Field crops	27	57	84	16
Livestock products	22	31	53	47
Agricultural output	24	44	68	32

[1] Includes a number of small state-owned agricultural enterprises such as model farms and experimental farms, not classed as state farms.

2. AVERAGE MANHOURS REQUIRED TO PRODUCE 100 POUNDS OF FARM PRODUCT: US 1956 AND USSR 1956-57	MANHOURS PER 100 POUNDS OF PRODUCTION		
	US FARMS	USSR STATE FARMS	USSR COLLECTIVE FARMS
Grain	0.45	0.85	3.31
Potatoes	0.45	1.91	2.31
Sugarbeets	0.22	0.95	1.41
Cotton (unginned)	8.52	13.52	19.41
Milk	2.13	4.50	6.66
Livestock: (Gain in weight)			
Cattle	3.58	23.58	50.80
Swine	2.86	19.50	46.72

SOURCE: US Department of Agriculture, *Soviet Agriculture Today* (1963), pages 10 and 31.

Schultz gives these reasons:[1]

1. The distorting influence of *industrial fundamentalism,* a feature of Marxist economic growth theory, holding that "industry is always the basic sector in achieving economic growth, that farm people are not only bound by tradition but are innately more backward that non-farm people" and that a substantial part of the farm labor force is in fact idle and contributes nothing to the national output.

2. Inefficiencies arising from the *doctrine of gigantic farms,* a conception of agricultural production for which Marxist thought has a strong bias. This concept "rests on the elemental belief of the superiority and necessity of large producing units . . . a proposition to the effect that large farms can produce farm products at less real cost than either small or medium-sized farms."

3. Suppression of incentives following upon the *doctrine that farmers do not respond normally to normal economic incentives.* "All manner of price and income policies can be and are promulgated under this doctrine. If it is true that farmers do not respond to prices, why not keep farm product prices low and thus reduce the costs of food while a country develops its industry? Compulsory deliveries of farm products of course follow, and by then the economic incentives required for efficient agricultural production have been greatly impaired."

4. Distortions and suppression of incentives due to *suppression of rental income from agricultural land.* "Once rent has been suppressed, sundry *ad hoc* measures are used to capture the value productivity of land and its appurtenances such as compulsory deliveries of farm products at some nominal price, the sale of farm products to the state at a low fixed price, and assessments against collective farms for welfare purposes."

5. Inefficiencies inherent in *absentee ownership.* "It is of the

---

[1] Theodore W. Schultz, head of the Department of Economics at the University of Chicago, in the previously cited *Transforming Traditional Agriculture.* The quotations from Professor Schultz' book focus on his findings with respect to Soviet agriculture. The book is concerned with the problems of improving the agriculture of the low income country in general. See also Schultz' *Big Tractors and Many Hoes, a Comment on Soviet Agriculture,* University of Chicago, Office of Agricultural Research, Paper 6006 (1960), or, in brief form under the same title in *Saturday Review,* January 21, 1961.

essence of state ownership that some of the basic decisions in farming are made under absentee conditions. . . . Absentee ownership in agriculture . . . is in general inefficient (because) the current operating decisions and the investment decisions in farming are not only subject to many small changes which entail spatial, seasonal, mechanical and biological subtleties that cannot be routinized, but also constantly require the adoption of new, superior, (factors of agricultural production) that are developed as a consequence of the advance of useful knowledge."

Schultz adds:

> . . . in a Soviet-type state, state ownership of land is only a detail in the totality of the controls the state has of agricultural production . . . the adverse effects of the absentee component inherent in state ownership . . . is compounded by other and much stronger instruments of control.
> . . . in the Soviet Union large power-driven machinery has been forced to the extreme. By tailoring agriculture to big tractors, it has forced agriculture into an absurd, bimodal structure of farm sizes, i.e., exceedingly large state and collective farms and tiny plot farms[1], a bimodal structure based on big tractors and many hoes. Both types are highly inefficient.
> . . . as far as one can tell presently the rate of acceptance of a new (factor of agricultural production, such as new technology, the better use of fertilizer, etc.) by farmers is best explained by the profitability of adopting and using the factor. . . . Tenure arrangements, including the variant adopted in the Soviet Union (complete state ownership of land), that determines how landlords and farmers share costs and returns can block the acceptance of factors that would be highly profitable under more appropriate arrangements.[2]

Thus, the difficulties of agriculture under Marxist government are to a great extent products of the Marxist view of things: industrial fundamentalism insisting upon intense concentration upon industry, making agriculture pay the bill through low food prices and low investment in agriculture; the inappropriate carryover from industry into agriculture of the idea that efficiency always grows with the scale of operations, leading to a farm

---

[1] *Soviet Agriculture Today* says that in 1962 collective farms averaged 15,500 acres of agricultural land and that state farms averaged 70,000 acres with an average of 25,000 acres sown to crops. Private plots averaged less than one acre.
[2] *Transforming Traditional Agriculture,* pp. 121 et seq. (parenthetical matter supplied).

structure composed of farms that are either too big or too small to be efficient; the depletion of incentives attendant upon Marxist seizure of title to the land; and resistance to technological progress arising from indifference on the part of the farmer caused by poor incentives and the fact that he is merely a tenant working for the absentee-owner-state.

In the early post-Stalin years, the USSR made strenuous efforts to slip out of the Marxist agricultural trap. The first effort was the New Lands program, initiated in 1954. Under this program, no less than some 100 million acres — equal to nearly a third of *total* US cropland acreage — of abandoned or theretofore unplowed land in Siberia, Kazakhstan and European Russia was brought into grain production. The move was heavily criticized in Russia and out, because the short growing season and the undependability of rainfall in this semi-arid region made some years of crop failure certain, and erosion a danger. It was apparently reasoned that the risk was worthwhile if bad years did not much outnumber good years and if the scale of the experiment was great enough to add large amounts to Russian grain stocks in the good years.

The second program was a plan for radically increasing corn production. Since only Western Russia has a growing season long enough for corn,[1] USSR corn output could be radically increased only if a major part of Russia's bread grain production could be transferred from Western Russia to the New Lands, releasing West Russian land for planting to corn. The corn was wanted as the basis for improvement of the most backward sector of all in Soviet agriculture, livestock production.

Thus, the New Lands program and the West Russian corn program were two parts of a plan aimed at solving the problem of improving the quality as well as the quantity of the diet in the leading Marxist society, by the introduction of more meats, milk and butter. That this is a problem absolutely requiring remedial action is indicated by the following.

1. Taking Soviet agriculture as a whole, per capita output was prob-

---

[1] Actually, long enough only to mature corn, for the most part, to the point of green silage for cattle feed.

ably *no higher* at the time of Stalin's death (1953) than when planned economic development began in Russia in 1928.

2. And, in 1953, Russian per capita consumption of livestock products was substantially below the 1928 level.

From 1952 through 1962 Soviet agricultural output expanded, according to USSR estimates, by about 60 per cent, and per capita Soviet farm production rose by 35 per cent. About five sixths of the gain took place in the years 1953-58.

After 1958, Soviet agriculture showed its old tendency to lag. The Russian government and the CPSU instituted a new round of reforms and reorganizations.

The first of these was the breakup in 1958 of the costly and inefficient Machine Tractor Stations. Through the years the MTS had insured Party-State control of the technically self-owned collectives by keeping and operating the heavy machinery used on collectives, even though the collective farm was strong enough to justify owning its own capital equipment. Breaking up the MTS increased the efficiency with which Russia's farms could use Russia's stock of agricultural machinery. But the collectives were forced to *buy* the machinery from the MTS, and some of the price came out of peasant incomes. The Soviet government had to extend the maximum period for payment for the machinery from five to ten years.

Attempts were made to alleviate the worst price and income exploitation of the peasantry in 1953-57 and in 1962, by increases in the prices paid by the government to collectives. The 1962 attack on this problem was drastic. Prices paid collectives for livestock and poultry were raised by 35 per cent, and butter and cream purchase prices rose by 10 and 5 per cent. These increases were passed on to the Soviet consumers. But this probably still did not make producing these things actually profitable.[1] However, to-

---

[1] Writing as one of a symposium of Western experts on the Soviet economy ten years after Stalin's death, Naum Jasny, dean of American economists specializing on the USSR economy, said in *Survey,* No. 47, April, 1963: "The expectation that production costs of animal products would decline (in the USSR) did not materialize ... so the prices paid to the kolkhozy (collective farms) on state procurements of animal products were raised by not less than 35 per cent on all meats on the average, by 29 per cent specifically on hogs, as from 1, June, 1962. But, *at least on beef, pork and poultry, the new procurement prices, high as they are, are lower than production costs* ... The fact that the output of animal products continued to rise, although slowly, in recent years, in spite of great losses incurred by the producers, is an indication of the amount of force exerted on the kolkhozy." (Emphasis supplied.)

gether with other measures taken to increase peasant incomes, the 1962 price rises were expected to raise collective farm income by some 15 to 20 per cent above what it was in 1961.[1] State farm wages were also raised.

Meanwhile, there were almost continual administrative re-organizations, in the hope that a new combination of control would be hit upon that would somehow overcome the effects of absentee landlordism on the Soviet scale. By early 1964, there was a definite edging toward more authority for the farm operator in Russia, and less for the Party bureaucrat. But movement in this direction appeared to be too slight to have much effect upon the massive inefficiencies imposed by the Soviet system.

Russia's scheme for growing its bread grains in the New Lands of the East, and shifting its warmer Western lands to corn so as to create the basis for large scale, lower cost meat and dairy output suffered disaster in 1962-63. Bad weather in successive years in the New Lands almost wiped out production there, and erosion following upon plowing up the sod threatened even longer term damage. It was announced that if, as, and when more reliable grain growing areas could be developed, the more treacherous parts of the New Lands would be turned back to grass. Russia was forced to join Red China in the US, Canadian, Australian and other Western grain markets. Russia's purchases came to between 11 and 12 million tons in 1963. The East European communist countries, which had been getting 3.5 to 4 million tons of grain from Russia yearly were also forced to buy grain from the West.[2]

These grain purchases used up great quantities of scarce supplies of foreign exchange, and caused Russia to sell some $400 million worth of gold by the end of November, 1963.[3] The foreign exchange and the gold that went for food imports subtracted from the ability of the USSR to purchase urgently needed machinery and consumer goods from the West. The grain failure

---

[1] *Dimensions of Soviet Economic Power*, p. 110.

[2] Better weather produced a good New Lands harvest in 1964, but it was the only good harvest since 1958, the intervening years being middling to bad. New Lands success depends on good years outweighing poor ones.

[3] Bank for International Settlements, *Press Review*, No. 235, April 12, 1963, Basle, Switzerland. Russia had been selling about half this much a year.

also denied foreign exchange earnings to the USSR: since 1959 Russia had been selling some 1.5 million tons of wheat abroad, outside the Bloc, each year.[1]

The grain crop failure of 1962-63 dramatized the fact that the long-term abuse and neglect of agriculture under Marxism in Russia had, by the end of the 1950s, come home to roost. The day of reckoning had been put off several years by initial gains in the New Lands, due simply to harvesting more acreage. The failure of the New Lands program put things back where they were in 1954: *Russia has a low-yield, low-efficiency agriculture that is slowly but surely clamping a strangle hold upon her general ability to advance economically.*

The effects had been long in showing up in a general way because the USSR set out in the 1920s with a fair industrial base, an agriculture that for the times was not too backward and a fairly sparse and slowly increasing population. Throughout the first decades of communism Russia was able to squeeze surplus product from her agriculture and use it for the benefit of industry (at the price of intense suffering in the countryside and at the cost of a barely sufficient diet throughout the country). As people moved from the country to the city to man the USSR's growing industrial-military complex it had been possible to feed them, and to keep the cost of food relatively low.

So long as the USSR had idle or semi-idle manpower in the countryside that could be siphoned off as needed for industry, the neglect and abuse of agriculture did not reveal itself as a general economic weakness, and Lenin's dictum that communism should be thought of as electrification plus Soviet power could be pursued in ideological serenity. But a potential strangle hold was all the while being created: the productivity of USSR agriculture was increasing only slowly. This meant that when the countryside's idle had all been moved to the city, Russia would find itself hard up for manpower for the further growth of its industry, because low productivity growth in agriculture would be releasing only a trickle, instead of the required torrent, of men from farm tasks for city tasks.

We have seen that it takes Russia from twice to seven times

---

[1] *Soviet Agriculture Today*, p. 58.

as many man-hours to produce 100 pounds of grain as it takes in the United States, and that it takes Russian farmers half again to twice again as much time to produce 100 pounds of cotton as is the case in this country. These and other differences in farm efficiency add up to the main fact: Russia uses over ten times as many farmers as does the United States. The United States reduced its agricultural labor force, from 1940 through 1961, over 42 per cent, from 9,540,000 to 4,463,000. Meanwhile, the USSR agricultural labor force declined by only 23 per cent, from 62,700,000 to 48,100,000. In 1962, the USSR still had over 22 per cent of its population in its farm labor force, down from 37 per cent in 1939. From 1940 to 1961, the US farm labor force declined, as a per cent of population, from 7 per cent to just under 3 per cent.[1]

The ineffectiveness of agriculture in Russia has now become an actively limiting factor on Russia's ability to make further economic progress:

> The reduced pace of Soviet growth (from 1958 onwards) can be explained in part by examining three sectors which originate over 80 per cent of GNP — industry, agriculture and services. During the 1958-62 period industrial output was increasing by somewhat more than 7 per cent a year, compared with over 10 per cent for the preceding eight years. Agricultural production has nearly stagnated, compared to an annual growth of over 5 per cent in the previous period (due chiefly to increased New Lands acreage). The services have moved contrary to the general trend, rising over 4 per cent a year compared with only about 1 per cent for earlier years.
> There has been a noticeable decline in the rate of increase in per capita consumption, largely the result of stagnation in farm output . . .[2]

If indeed Russian agriculture must remain a stepchild in the Marxist view of things, then improvement of Russia's farm output must remain difficult and probably slow and small. However, it has become increasingly clear to the Russian leadership that the agricultural soft spot is a danger to, and a limitation upon, all

---

[1] USSR labor force, *Soviet Agriculture Today,* page 28; USSR population, *Annual Economic Indicators for the U.S.S.R.,* previously cited, p. 3; US labor force, US Department of Commerce, *Statistical Abstract of the United States 1963,* page 219; U.S. population, same, p. 5.

[2] *Annual Economic Indicators for the U.S.S.R.,* p. 91.

Russia's economic plans. It is clear that the rise in the Russian standard of living cannot proceed very far unless the per capita provision of foods and fibers can increase radically. With its agriculture so weak, the USSR cannot hope to match, much less to surpass, United States per capita output of farm products, and would probably be prevented from ever overtaking us in industrial production. An uncertain food supply, an uncertain and relatively expensive supply of industrial farm products, plus the continued imprisonment of about half the Russian labor force in agriculture, menace the continued rapid expansion of Russian industry and threaten to cause Russian industrial production to continue to be a high cost affair.

Russia could not, under these circumstances, become the cheap and plentiful producer of capital (not to speak of consumer) goods she needs to become if she is to maintain herself at the pinnacle of Marxist economic achievement, and keep her image as a model for imitation by the underdeveloped countries of the free world.

In the near future there will be big increases in fertilizer production, and possibly large-scale irrigation projects. There will certainly be continued organizational writhings. But beyond such temporizing, there would appear to be a time, not far off, when the Russian Marxist leadership must make a basic decision about Soviet agriculture.[1] It is hard to see how one or some combination of the following changes could long be avoided:

---

[1] Soon after new leaders replaced Khrushchov in the USSR, the new CPSU First Secretary, Leonid I. Brezhnev, announced that more recognition and scope would be given to private plot farming in the Soviet Union. He said (*New York Times,* November 5, 1964):

> "It would be wrong to disregard the potential of private plots cultivated by collective farmers, industrial workers and office employees to satisfy their personal requirements.
> "Unwarranted limitations have been imposed in this sphere in recent years, despite the fact that economic conditions have not been ripe for such a step. These limitations have now been removed."

The *New York Times* dispatch added:

> "Details of the government's new policy toward private farming were becoming available even before Mr. Brezhnev announced the over-all decision. Newspapers arriving from the Ukraine and Estonia carried decrees cancelling past limitations on the sizes of private plots and on livestock holdings . . . Mr. Brezhnev emphasized that increases in consumption confronted the leadership with the task of overcoming the lag in agricultural output:
> " 'We will have to continue to increase capital investments in agriculture and in the industries that supply it with machines and fertilizers.' "

1. A decision to turn agriculture in Russia, or a major share of it, back to essentially free enterprise, competitive operation, i.e., a large increase in the role of the "private plots" which now do so much on so little.

2. A decision to alter the basic proportions in Marxist economic development as exemplified by the USSR, depriving industry of a significant part of the investment of funds and talent that now goes into it, in favor of achieving economic balance and greater underlying strength by greatly increasing agricultural investment and incomes.

3. A decision to keep things as they are — taxing agriculture to finance the military-industrial complex — and adopt long range plans for making up Russia's agricultural deficiencies as capitalist countries make up theirs, by trade.

Going Fast More Slowly: Industry

Escaping from the dead hand of the ruling doctrine without disowning it too explicitly has been developed into a truly fine art in the Khrushchov era.[1]

Sweeping changes in the planning system are quite unavoidable. . . . Essential features of a new system would be more flexible use of prices, increased significance of the profit motive, the partial replacement of material allocations by free purchases, by contract between enterprises, greater enterprise autonomy in deciding by reference to commercial orders, and so on. The 64,000 ruble questions is: can such a decentralized system at the 'micro' level be reconciled with centralized 'macro' planning?[2]

One may suppose that in the long run the new (mathematical computer) techniques will enable the Soviet planner to evolve at least an approximation to a trial-and-error quest for the best plan solution, and substitute it for what today is not much more than a groping in the dark. The penalty for backwardness in this field has been dramatized by the Gosplan (state planning agency) journal, where it is estimated that, should the present methods be perpetuated, by 1980 the whole adult population would have to be employed in planning calculations

---

[1] Alfred Zauberman, in *Survey*, No. 47, April, 1963.

[2] Alec Nove, in *Survey*, No. 47, April, 1963.

and controls. A novel and remarkable variant of the vision of full communism.[1]

The agricultural failure threatening to fetter the entire Soviet economy is due in great part to the fixation of all Soviet governments from Lenin's onwards upon industrial development. Lenin said that "Communism is Soviet power plus the electrification of the entire country."[2] The much quoted saying sums up the nearly singleminded drive of Russian Marxism to build up the nation's non-agricultural side, the "industrial fundamentalism" that has led to chronic agricultural weakness in the Marxist society.

The corollary, and in some sense justification, of Russia's agricultural failure, therefore, should be very great industrial progress. And that is the case: Russia has risen under Marxism from her place as the world's fifth ranking industrial power in 1913[3] to the second ranking today (or, third ranking if the comparison is made of the Soviet economy with the economies of the six nations of the European Economic Community grouped as a single economy).

A study prepared for the US Congress compared pre-Marxist with post-Marxist growth in Russia. It came to the conclusion

Bibliographical Note: The US Congress and the sovietological journals took the decade mark after Stalin's death as a convenient point for summing up what, in retrospect, Stalin's economic bequest to Russia had been, and what Stalin's successors did with it. See *Dimensions of Soviet Economic Power; Problems of Communism,* Vol. XII; *Survey,* Nos. 47 and 48; *Studies on the Soviet Union,* Vol. II, Nos. 1 and 3.

[1] Zauberman, as before.

[2] Quoted, to pick an official Russian source from among many users, in *USSR Today and Tomorrow,* Foreign Languages Publishing House, Moscow, 1959, p. 100.

[3] Soviet Handbook, *1959-1965,* (Soviet Booklets, 3 Rosary Gardens, London), p. 6. The *Bulletin* of the Institute for the Study of the USSR, Munich, November, 1962, made a study of economic growth in Russia 1870-1910 showing that industrialization in Russia was very rapid in this period (steel output started about equal to that of France in 1870 and was just slightly ahead of France in 1910). This would indicate a No. 4 or No. 5 position for Russia among the industrial nations just before World War I. The comparison of US and USSR industrial production by G. Warren Nutter in the 1959 study of the Soviet economy, done for the Joint Economic Committee of the US Congress, *Comparisons of the United States and Soviet Economies* indicates (Page 105) that the United States and Czarist Russia had almost identical (and very high) industrial growth rates from 1870 to 1913: 5.3 per cent per year for Russia and 5.1 per cent for the US. This and many other studies tend to show that when Marxism took over in Russia in 1918, it could build upon an extensive industrial foundation including a railway network, a steel industry the equal to that of France, and an extensive machine building industry, plus a sizeable skilled labor force. Communist literature tends to swell the Marxist achievement in Russia by representing pre-revolutionary Russia as having been nearly undeveloped industrially.

that in the last 40 years of Czarist government Russia's industrial growth averaged 5.3 per cent per year (1870-1913) while from the beginning of Soviet planned economic growth in 1928 through 1955, comparable Russian civilian industrial output rose at 6.1 per cent a year.[1] This, and other key before and after comparisons, plus comparisons with US experience, are summarized in Table 4.

This is instructive in how hard a goal the USSR has set itself in trying to overtake the United States within a fairly short time. From 1928 through 1955 Russian industrial output grew about two thirds faster, *per year* than did US industrial output. Since then the USSR growth advantage has persisted in most years, although it has declined lately (Table 1). But, despite three decades of large annual gains, Russia's industry is *still* far smaller than ours, for two main reasons: 1) The United States industrial base was much bigger than Russia's in 1928, and 2) as Table 4 shows, US industrial *efficiency* rose over the 1928-55 period at a rate nearly a fifth higher than the improvement of efficiency in USSR factories and mines.

This glance at history brings us to the question: what has been happening lately?

In Table 1 we see the basic data. We have remarked that Russia's performance under Marxist control has been good, but was by no means unexcelled among capitalist nations. Marxism has evidently not taught Russia any economic secrets: it has not dissolved away any of the basic problems of economic development, because it has not been able to alter the ingredients of the economic growth culture. Any nation with equal determination and command over comparable economic resources can do as well or better, and do it without the horrors of police coercion.

Table 1 records the growth of the USSR economy as a whole, including Russia's lagging agricultural sector. What about industry only, to single out the sector to which the USSR from its inception has given consecrated attention? A 1962 study made for the United States Congress said:

[1] G. Warren Nutter in *Comparisons of the United States and the Soviet Economies, Joint Economic Committee, US Congress, (Part I, page 105).* Nutter adds, Page 116, that Soviet industrial output in 1928 approximately equalled that of the United States in 1877, and in 1955, USSR industrial output equalled that of the United States in 1913.

The best trained and highest quality manpower as well as a large and rapidly growing share of investment have been directed annually into industry, and primarily into heavy industry whose principal end products are (1) armaments, and (2) machinery and construction materials required for more investment and more industrial capacity.[1]

Average annual growth of industrial production in the long period from 1937 through 1961 was higher in Russia than in the other principal industrial countries (Table 5). However, all the principal industrial nations had high rates of gain in industrial production over this period. Russia was not the leader in the 1950s. In the decade following 1950, Japan was even more of a nonpareil in industrial growth than in overall economic growth. Japan's industry grew half again as fast as did the Soviet Union's in 1950-55, and by more than twice the Soviet rate in the 1955-1961 years. West Germany matched the USSR for the whole 1950-1961 period, and Italy's rate of progress in industrialization was quite close to Russia's.

What happened, meanwhile, inside Russia? The first line of Table 6 shows that Russian industrial expansion tended during the 1950s and early 1960s to go more slowly, although still fast. There was a slowdown, but nothing like the steep downturn of GNP (where the agricultural production disaster figures). There are reasons for both the continued fast growth of USSR industry and for the fact that it has slowed.

First, the factors that have made the Soviet economy, especially its industry, a fast growth economy. Here there is a group of long term factors, and another group of influences that gave Russia special shorter term growth impetus during the 1950s. We will look first at the longer term factors.

One of the strongest long term growth advantages is the advantage of being backward, if you are trying to do something about your backwardness. The Joint Economic Committee of the Congress, seeking the facts about Soviet Russia's economic growth in 1959, was advised that this is discernible not only for the whole economy, but by industries:

---

[1] Rush V. Greenslade and Phyllis Wallace, in *Dimensions of Soviet Economic Power*, p. 119.

There has been a rather striking inverse relation between the rapidity of growth in an industry over the Soviet period (of time in Russia) and its "stage of development" at the beginning of the period. For a sample of 48 industries, those whose outputs were smallest relative to the United States in 1913 have shown a strong tendency to grow fastest.[1]

One of the main advantages of backwardness lies in the fact that the backward economy, or industry, can make quick, large additions to its rate of output simply by acquiring and putting to use foreign technology. The tractor can be copied and built, rather than developed. Automation of whole industries can be copied. The tedious stage-by-stage development of the original technological advance is saved. The highest known technology can be put to work at one fell swoop. The capital cost of acquiring ready-made technology is probably very much less than the cost of developing it. Precious capital as well as precious time is saved, by comparison with the costs in money and time of the original development. Soviet Russia has been buying (or otherwise acquiring abroad, as in the case of nuclear technology) foreign technology and putting it to work on a massive scale since the early 1930s. The extent of the benefits is probably most clearly indicated by the results in agriculture, where new technology has not been so extensively acquired and put to use. There, for reasons we saw in the preceding section, Soviet Russia has not been able to modernize as much as she has in industry. Agriculture has stagnated, over the long term, while Soviet industry has grown fast, fed by massive injections of foreign technology and the devotion of Russia's best inventive and managerial talent.

The second major factor in Russia's fast industrial growth also stems from the advantage of being backward, if non-industrialization is taken to mean backwardness (as it is taken in Russia). This is the fact that at the outset of the communization of Russia, the country's manpower was largely in agriculture. Consequently, even small increases in agricultural efficiency have tended to release large numbers of people who could move off the land into the cities and join the industrial labor force. Over the past half century, Russia's city population has grown much faster than the

[1] G. Warren Nutter, in *Comparisons of the United States and Soviet Economies,* Part I, p. 100.

nation's total population. From 1926 through 1961, Russia's total population grew by 73 millions, while its urban population grew 86 millions. During the 1950s, the total population grew 14 per cent while the urban population increased over 40 per cent.[1] That is, Russia has been transferring workers on a mass scale from the farm to industry. This better deployment of the labor force has been one of the chief growth factors in Western countries, as they industrialized. It has served Russia likewise. Since at the outset of the 1960s Russia's population was still about half rural, Russia still has gains to come from shifting manpower from farming to industry, although not such great gains as in the past.

Russia has capitalized these long term advantages of backwardness by devoting a very high proportion of its total production to investment, chiefly in industry. By depriving the Soviet consumer, in favor of satiating the Soviet machine industry, and by using all the surplus value that could be squeezed out of agriculture to buy tools, machines and technological advice abroad and to feed Russia's cities, Russia under Marxism has rapidly expanded the size of its industrial plant and equipment. In so doing, the USSR was providing high productivity machinery for the labor of men and women who only a while before had been semi-idle farm hands. The growth of non-agricultural employment is the key index here, and non-agricultural employment grew by about half in Russia in the 1950s.

> In other words, the Soviet economy has been growing rapidly by devoting a very large proportion of its resources to investment favoring economic growth, and by rapidly shifting the structure of its labor force in favor of the high-productivity sectors. Under these conditions, the USSR has in the past been able to achieve high growth rates without paying principal attention to the efficiency or balance with which it was converting resources into over-all economic growth.[2]

---

[1] James W. Brackett, in *Dimensions of Soviet Economic Power,* pp. 511-512.

[2] Gregory Grossman in *Survey,* No. 47. This description of the sources of Soviet growth is indebted to Professor Grossman's analyses in *Survey,* No. 47, 1963, and *Problems of Communism,* Vol. XII, No. 2, 1963, as well as to his earlier articles in *Problems of Communism.* Acknowledgement is also due to Wolfgang Leonhard in *Problems of Communism,* XII/2, and to Peter Wiles, Abram Bergson, Alec Nove and Alfred Zauberman in *Survey,* No. 47. No transfer of responsibility to any of these sources of expert knowledge about the USSR is intended.

A number of other — mainly shorter-term — factors tended to support the Soviet growth curve, through about mid-1958. After that point unfavorable factors, chiefly the previous lack of emphasis upon economic efficiency and the imbalance of industrial and agricultural development, began increasingly to be evident.

The special, mainly shorter-term, factors working for a high rate of industrial expansion in Russia in most of the 1950s can be summarized as follows:

1. Under Stalin, an enormous accumulation of Russian productive capital and human resources was made ready for use. But the terror, general chaos in construction and training, the destructiveness of the collectivization drive, World War II, and lack of rationality in incentives prevented effective use of the newly accumulated resources. In the 1950s there was a general shaking down of the mechanism of production. The productive capacities and skills acquired in the 30s and 40s were assimilated, cross connected, and put to better use.

2. There was still very much foreign technology to be taken over, and Russia took it into the Soviet economy on a vast scale, partly from the satellite countries of East Europe.

3. Some administrative and policy rigidities in use of resources were loosened to good effect. Such were the shift away from the use of coal and to petroleum and natural gas; increased emphasis on the chemicals industry (related to the increased production of oil and gas); the acceptance of automation. In 1957 the central economic ministries that had directed the whole economy were broken up and their functions (except planning) were given to some 100 regional economic authorities (sovnarkhozes).

4. There were some one-time-for-always gains, chiefly the liberation for useful employment of a large but untold number of political prisoners.

5. Throughout the 50s (up to mid-1961) the percentage share of defense in Soviet outlays was steadily reduced, winding up at only about half what it was at the outset of the period.

6. Russian policy makers were permitted to let their thoughts wander

toward economic realism, though Marxist doctrine still set definite limits to the search for and use of rational solutions to economic problems.

7. Agriculture increased its total output by half from 1953 through 1958, chiefly through a vast increase in grains grown on newly planted acreage in the Eastern New Lands.

All this brought on inside Russia a wave of good feeling, optimism and renewed confidence. In the outer world, it inspired surprise and some dismay that the disheveled Marxist giant seemed after so many years of fumbling to have pulled himself together and, quite suddenly, to have emerged as a going, modern mechanism able to make a coordinated effort and get rapid and large results. Per capita income rose sharply in Russia, both in the city and in the country. The agricultural upsurge not only helped income in the countryside; it also buoyed industry. Meanwhile, industry continued to be stimulated by the accustomed large inflow of resources resulting from the traditional concentration of investment on industry. Industrial growth was further encouraged by savings and efficiencies resulting from the 1957 administrative reorganization.

The 1953-58 economic gains seemed at last to be paying in rapid progress for a generation of suffering and privation under Marxism. The optimism this generated was reflected in the Seven Year Plan, adopted in January, 1959, for the further rapid economic development of Russia in the period 1959-1965.

The Plan was said to inaugurate the period of "full construction of communist society" — that ideal society of economic abundance and full social harmony envisioned by Marx as the ultimate stage of human history. Supposedly the Plan would boost the Soviet economy most of the way toward the goal of overtaking and surpassing the United States in per capita production and consumption — a point which would finally be reached around 1970, clinching the "historic victory of socialism over capitalism" on our planet.[1]

But the bubbling-over claims of the Seven Year Plan (and its goals) were later toned down. This was done at the 22nd

---

[1] Grossman, *Problems of Communism,* Vol. XII, No. 2, April, 1963, p. 36.

Congress of the Russian Communist Party, in October, 1961, which adopted the New Program (of the CPSU) we have previously mentioned. When the New Program came to be closely examined, it seemed to have stretched over a longer future much of the progress toward "that ideal society of economic abundance" anticipated in 1958 for the next 10 or 12 years. The New Program marched on, from 1970 to 1980, calling in this much longer period, only for building the *"foundations* of communism." That is, under the New Program the target is only to get ready, by 1980, to produce soon thereafter the "society of economic abundance and full social harmony."

This is a considerable contrast in modesty with the expectations of the Seven Year Plan, as officially described:

> The principal task of the Seven Year Plan for the development of the national economy of the USSR in 1959-65 is to bring about a further mighty advance in all branches of the economy on the basis of the priority expansion of heavy industry, and a substantial rise in the country's economic potential with the aim of ensuring a steady improvement in the living standards of the people. . . .
>
> The fulfillment of this plan will be a decisive step towards creating the material and technical foundations of communism and accomplishing the main economic task of the USSR — to overtake and surpass the most highly developed capitalist countries in per capita output within a historically brief space of time. . . .
>
> . . . if we reckon per head of population, said Khrushchov at the 21st Congress of the CPSU, it will probably take us another five years after completing the Seven Year Plan to overtake and surpass the United States in industrial production. Consequently, by that time — or even earlier — the Soviet Union will rank first in the world both for physical volume of production and production per head of the population.[1]

---

[1] *Soviet Handbook,* 1959-1965 pp. 30 & 31, where the following Seven Year Plan output targets are officially given:

(per cent increases)

National income	62-65
Total industrial output	80
Total agricultural output	70
Productivity of labor:	
In industry	45-50
On collective farms	100
On state farms	60-65
In construction	60-65
In railway transport	34-37
Real incomes of the population	40
Retail trade	62

But after 1958, just when the last touches were being put to the Seven Year Plan, the upthrust of the Soviet economy slacked off substantially. This is visible in Table 6.

What happened? We have already noted the tendency of agricultural stagnation to choke off general economic progress in the USSR. But there were downward influences specific to industry.

As noted, some of the special growth advantages Russia had in the 1950s were one-shot stimulants (such as the release for productive employment of political prisoners, and industrial reorganization). Much more importantly, Russia was beginning to exhaust some of the advantages of backwardness. As her level of technological knowledge and use approached nearer to the highest level in the world, there was less (even though still much) that Russia could transfer. Especially, there were likely to be fewer of the big, fast-gain technological plums to be plucked, since the best had been the first plucked. In this, and in all other respects "production in the USSR as elsewhere is subject to diminishing returns."[1] There is no special, unflagging, Marxist growth.

There were other depressants. Due to Russia's tremendous losses of life in World War II, the young adult addition to the labor force became less favorable to Russia in the late 1950s than it had been. Meantime, stepped up investment plans, USSR participation in foreign aid on a sizeable scale, the effort to improve living standards within Russia, and the USSR space exploration effort put new pressures on the nation's productive facilities. At the same time, Russia pushed to completion a reduction of the standard work week, outside agriculture, from 48 to 40 hours. Finally, the many reforms and reorganizations installed by Khrushchov exacted a toll for their initial benefits: Russia's vast, self-protective bureaucracy learned how to carry on old practices under new tables of organization. New rigidities began to appear, and new administrative weaknesses showed up.

In 1961, there was an added factor. The USSR suddenly increased its military outlays considerably, reversing the favor-

---

[1] Abram Bergson, *Survey*, No. 47.

able effects of the downtrend in military production felt through-out the 1950s.

Summing up in the light of developments in the Soviet Union through 1963, a study for the Joint Economic Committee of the US Congress said:[1]

The Soviet Union appears to have entered upon a period of secular deceleration in its growth following 1958. In the period 1950-1958 its national product rose by an annual average of 6.8 per cent, second only to West Germany among the major industrial economies. In no year since 1958 has this rate been attained and the average for the past four years has been only 4.6 per cent, below the growth of Japan, Italy and West Germany, and equal to that of France. Even if the unfavorable year of 1958 for the market economies be omitted from the comparison, the secular deceleration in growth has been far sharper for the USSR than for the other major economies. On a per capita basis, the perform-ance of the Soviet economy is even less favorable, in recent years being below Japan and the large continental economies.

During the 1958-62 period industrial output was increasing by some-what more than 7 per cent per year compared with over 10 per cent for the preceding eight years. Agricultural production has nearly stag-nated, compared to an annual growth of over 5 per cent in the pre-vious period. The services have moved contrary to the general trend, rising over 4 per cent a year compared with only about 1 per cent for the earlier years.

If provisional information for 1963 is introduced, an even slower growth than for 1962 appears. Part of the explanation for the decline in the rate of growth lies in a less favorable manpower situation, the rate of increase in employment having declined to 1.3 per cent from 1.7 per cent, but more striking has been the declining rate of produc-tivity advancement, even if cyclical weather influences are removed. In this respect too, the reduction in the Soviet rate of increase is the largest of the seven (major industrial) countries.

There has been a noticeable decline in the rate of increase in per capita consumption, largely the result of the stagnation in farm output and to a lesser extent because of the decline in new housing construction. . . . The rate of increase in investment also fell significantly, contrary to the experience of the other major economies. . . . Of equal importance is

---

[1] *Annual Economic Indicators for the U.S.S.R.*, pp. 91-93. Most of the developments sketched in these paragraphs are depicted, in numbers, in Table 1.

the sharply reduced rate of return on investment. In the earlier period the Soviet Union obtained about the same increase in output per employee from a unit of nonhousing investment as did France and Germany, though less than did Japan. Since 1958 the productivity of investment has been . . . the lowest of all major economies except the United Kingdom.

Soviet consumption levels are only a quarter of those of the United States, half those of France, Germany and the United Kingdom, and about 80 per cent of Italy's. . . . The really striking Soviet resource priority is found in defense. Its per capita level is two thirds as high as that of the United States and about double the average for France, Germany and Italy.

The Outlook:
One Touch of the Market

The USSR economy will continue to enjoy the benefits of much technological borrowing from the more advanced nations, though less and in smaller lumps than formerly. Its own technical skills will grow to offset much of the decline in cheap acquisition of ready-made foreign technology. Between 1962 and 1972, the *total* USSR labor force will grow in about the same proportion to population as it did between 1952 and 1962. But: "It seems unlikely that now, when it accounts for over half the active population, *non-agricultural* employment will expand proportionately as fast over the next decade as it did over the preceeding one."[1] So USSR industry will probably have to face up to a manpower shortage. This could be aggravated by any increases in the USSR military establishment. Further, Russia faces another demand upon the ability of the Soviet economy to increase its efficiency if its growth is not to slacken. This results from promises in the Seven Year Plan to reduce the standard workweek further in the later years of the Plan period, from 40 to 35 hours. If productivity does not increase rapidly, this promise will become difficult to keep. What shape the main economic trends will take in Russia in the near future depends upon the answers to a number of questions, such as those following.

---

[1] Grossman, *Survey,* No. 47.

To what extent will the USSR be forced by its desperate housing shortage to sacrifice some of the materials of industrial growth to build facilities for the production of construction materials? Will the Soviet educational reforms of the 1950s — designed to produce a carefully controlled number of elite specialists, and a fast growing mass of technicians and skilled labor — result in rapidly rising labor productivity, as intended? Can the heavy footed Soviet system take in automation quickly and put it to work on a large scale in a short time? Will Soviet women, who have contributed so much of Soviet Russia's daily work, be content to go on doing so, or will they demand that the regime pause in its efforts to overtake the US at least long enough to build street sweeping, materials handling, and other machinery to replace female labor? How much can investment in civilian industry, agriculture and transportation increase? Or, to turn this last question over, what demands will military production make upon Russian resources in coming years?

Nearly all these questions come down to the single query: how *productive* can the Soviet economy make itself in the further use of its growth advantages, and in overcoming its shortage problems? This, in turn, can be stated as the questions: can the leading Marxist society, with nearly half a century of experience in its planning files, learn to meet its needs and to use its opportunities by the exercise of ingenuity, rather than by the force of main strength? Can it become a high productivity (i.e., high efficiency), high quality economy, as well as a high growth economy?

The USSR cannot evade this question, for it cannot accomplish its high, hard objective by the exercise of main, awkward strength. If it were content to overtake the US in *size* of output, it could do so, because the USSR has a bigger population and more territory than does the United States (although, even in mere total production, Russia has far to go by comparison).

But the USSR has challenged its Marxist system to overtake and surpass the US in *per capita* output. That means *the Soviet system, to achieve its goal, must become more efficient than the United States system, for without doing so it cannot produce more per man, woman and child,* unless there are large differences in the size and makeup of the labor forces the two populations provide. There are no such differences big enough to permit Russia to overtake the US in per capita output without becoming more efficient in the production of goods and services than we are.

These questions are being taken very seriously indeed in the USSR, where CPSU leaders have made almost a profession of warning that future gains must come chiefly out of increases in productivity, that is, from more and ever more efficient allocation of economic resources and from more efficient production.[1]

Two streams of thought by Soviet economists have been converging in recent years toward something like the "market socialism" proposed in 1938 by the Polish economist and Marxist philosopher, Oskar Lange. The two basic ideas under consideration in Russia are the two halves of Lange's proposal for permitting the Marxist society to simulate capitalism's market economics.

The first is concerned with the role of prices in economic operations, and the second is concerned with the role of profits. The econometrician L. V. Kantorovich attracted attention in 1959 to the idea of letting prices play a bigger role in directing the economy. In proposing the programming of production (i.e., planning) by mathematical procedures, he stated that the correct solution of any economic planning problem could not be found without the use of prices that balanced supply with demand. Kantorovich described his "objectively determined" planning prices (which he proposed for use only by planners) as "shadow prices" a hypothetical use of prices familiar by the same name in the West. Shadows or reality, they set off controversy because they suggested letting prices, rather than planners following the Party's objectives, decide how much, of what, should be used for what purposes, where, and when, in the economy.

Second, in the autumn of 1962, *Pravda* gave official display to proposals by a Kharkov economist, Professor Ye. Liberman to use profitability (rather than success in meeting Plan goals) as the main index to the success or failure of a production enterprise. Shortly thereafter, Khrushchov gave encouragement to such criti-

---

[1] See Harry G. Shaffer, "What Price Economic Reforms?" and Rush V. Greenslade, "Khrushchev and the Economists" in *Problems of Communism,* Vol. XII, No. 3, June, 1963, to both of which the discussion here is indebted.

ques of the existing system by a vigorous denunciation before the CPSU Central Committee of industrial planning methods in use. This was followed by renewal, extension and combination of the Liberman and Kantorovich propositions for simulating the market through use of prices and profits.

> One cannot avoid the conclusion that supply-demand pricing would be the next objective of some "liberal" economists if the present proposals were adopted. This small logical step, however, would be enormous ideologically; the economists would be proposing, in effect, to substitute for central planning of enterprise outputs Adam Smith's "invisible hand" (the competitive forces of the market).
> ... the common characteristic of all the proposals is the search for impersonal and automatic rules to substitute for arbitrary or bureaucratic decision-making; a profitability rule for enterprises, a full cost rule for prices, or linear programming rules for central planning.[1]

As we have previously noted, this would be to accept the unacceptable: invasion of the full, final, unquestionable authority of the Communist Party by autonomous forces (prices, profits, competition) allowed to shape economic (and thereby political-social) decisions, without reference to the Party.

To sum up, Russia's need for greater economic efficiency is so intense that some changes aimed at achieving higher efficiency are inevitable; the Party leadership has permitted the idea to get about that Russia might consider adopting something like market socialism; at the same time there has been increasing discussion of the use of a device less embarrassingly an open simulation of the competitive market, a Kantorovich-like solution, in which mathematical-computer procedures would be used to play economic games designed to determine, within the privacy of the planning agency, what prices would achieve planned objectives without economic distortion.

Despite the pragmatism of the new men of Russian Marxism, they are likely to resist the market socialism solution as long as possible in favor of some solution that would not dilute Party authority:

> The Party man sees the problem (output must be raised). He goes directly to the worker, explains the goal and its importance, and wins

---

[1] Greenslade, *Problems of Communism*, XII/3, parenthetical matter added.

his confidence and enthusiasm. The worker then reveals a secret trick that can double output — a trick which he will adopt, provided that certain government bureaucrats leave him alone. The Party man chases away the bureaucrats, and the problem is solved.[1]

This caricature of Khrushchov's methods illustrates the essential problem in Russia: the still dominant mystic belief that there exists a Marxist dynamic that will solve everything, if it is only left free to operate.

But:

... the economic pressure for better management of resources is more likely to grow than to diminish. . . . Recent evidence indicates that the return on investment in Russia is declining — a situation that has come about partly as a penalty of success. . . . In the case of the Soviet Union, the rapid growth of its economy has been due to the large gap between the low level of technology in use and the high level in the West available for borrowing. As a result of 15 years of massive investment in the postwar period, the gap has narrowed, and gains from new technology are not coming as easily as before. In consequence, gains from organizational change appear to be more attractive than before.

If, as it now appears, party troubleshooting should prove to be an inadequate answer to increasingly subtle economic problems, some successor of Khrushchov's may decide that the interests of the party as a whole are better served by limiting the authority of the lower party levels through stricter rules. There appears to be only two choices in rules for economic administration: (1) a systematic hierarchy with appropriate definitions of mission and function, or (2) the rules of the market place, with profit maximization and prices equating supply and demand . . . bureaucratization or creeping capitalism.[2]

But there is a problem dimension beyond the matter of efficiency, critical as that is. This is qualitative improvement, a dimension in which the Marxist system may find it even harder to operate than in the dimension of material efficiency. With this area of difficulty in mind we can add the following to our previous questions on the shape of the future in the leading Marxist society:

Can a planning system reared on and geared to the amassing

---

[1] Greenslade, *Problems of Communism,* XII/3.

[2] Greenslade, *Problems of Communism,* XII/3. There might be a third possibility, which would stem from the first of Greenslade's two choices. This would be increasing centralization as a defense against any tendency for capitalism to creep in.

of economic resources for use in a relatively uncomplicated system of production emphasizing military and investment hardware, and insensitive to all else, change its fundamental ways? Can Soviet planners find a way, under Marxism, to adjust to the more complex and delicate task of developing an economic mechanism sensitive to the full range of human as well as national needs and desires? Can the Marxist command economy become a Marxist response economy, affable enough to learn of and cater to the multitudinous and conflicting (and sometimes growth negative) desires of its people for such things as pretty dresses, good housing, automobile transportation, nice furniture (and everything else — even cars? — that Communist Man will expect the affluent communist society to produce as well as the capitalist society produces)? Or, can the Marxist society be only an awkward giant, willy-nilly brutal, all nuts and bolts, no bells and bows?

That is, can Marxist planning simulate the workings of the capitalist market economy? Can Technological Man, weaned on the machine, Plan in hand, hatch the fully communist state, productive enough to rear a reasonably contented Communist Man, able to call upon his society for whatever he reasonably needs?

Table 1 · The USSR Economy Compared to Other Principal Industrial Economies 1950-1962

Country	Population 1962	Gross National Product 1962	Per Capita GNP	Rate of GNP Growth		
				1950/58 (Average)	1958-62 (Average)	1960-63 (Average)
Unit	Millions	Billion $5	Dollars [5]	Per Cent	Per Cent	Per Cent
France	47.6[1]	$ 83.6	$1,810	4.4%	4.8%	5.1%
Germany (West)	55.1[1]	96.2	1,780	7.6	6.2	3.9
Italy	50.3[1]	52.8	1,058	5.6	7.2	6.3
Japan	95.3[2]	77.0	811	6.1	13.2	10.2
United Kingdom	53.4[3]	91.5	1,730	2.4	2.8	2.4
United States	188.3[4]	551.8	3,004	2.9	4.3	3.8
USSR	223.1	256.3	1,158	6.8[6]	4.6[6]	3.5[6]

Country / Unit	Private Consumption		Fixed Investment			Defense		Other		Increases in Labor Productivity		Industrial Output per Employee 1962
	7	8	9	10	11	12	13	14	15	16	17	18
	Per Capita Uses of Gross National Product[7]											
	Dollars	Per Cent of Per Capita GNP	Dollars	Per Cent of Per Capita GNP 1962	1950-60	Dollars	Per Cent of Per Capita GNP	Dollars	Per Cent of Per Capita GNP	1950/58 Per Cent	1958/62 Per Cent	Dollars
France	$1,185	65.4%	$294	16.2%	20.6%	$108	5.9%	$223	12.3%	4.0%	3.8%	$ 4,000
Germany (West)	1,047	58.8	461	25.8	25.4	100	5.6	172	9.6	5.1	4.8	3,537
Italy	607	57.3	224	21.1	22.9	40	3.7	187	17.6	3.9	5.9	3,052
Japan	8		8		25.6	8		8		4.0	11.5	1,643
United Kingdom	1,098	63.4	283	16.3	16.8	125	7.2	224	12.9	1.9	2.0	3,772
United States	1,889	62.8	480	15.9	17.7	300	9.9	335	11.1	1.9	2.7	10,160
USSR	486	41.9	373	32.2	23.9[9]	192	16.6	107	9.2	5.0	3.3	3,531

Source: Except as indicated in footnotes, US Congress, Joint Economic Committee, *Annual Economic Indicators for the U.S.S.R.* 1964, as follows: Col. 1, p. 3; Cols. 2 and 3, p. 96; Cols. 4 and 5, p. 95; Col. 6, p. 98; Cols. 7-15, p. 95; Cols. 16 and 17, p. 95; Col. 18, p. 97.

[1] End of 1962; Source, OECD, *General Statistics*, September 1963, p. 33.

[2] End of 1962; Source, Government of Japan, Japanese Economic Statistics, March 1963, p. 67.

[3] Mid-1962. Source, see Footnote 1.

[4] Source, see Footnote 1.

[5] 1962 market prices.

[6] Adjusted for arms production (see also Table 6).

[7] 1962 market prices, except investments as per cent of per capita GNP, which are annual averages at factor cost of total capital investments; Source, Stanley H. Cohn in *Dimensions of Soviet Economic Power*, Joint Economic Committee, 1962, p. 82.

[8] Not available.

[9] The rate of growth of USSR investment declined from 10.8 per cent a year, 1950-58 to 7.7 per cent, 1958-62. See JEC, *Annual Economic Indicators*, p. 96.

Table 2

The Arithmetic of Economic Growth

	Per Year
Per Capita USSR Gross National Product, 1962	$1,158
USSR Economic Growth Rate to 1970, if the growth rate of 1950-58 is projected to 1970	6.8%
Less, Rate of growth of population in the USSR 1960/70	−1.2%
Rate of growth of per capita GNP, using above data	5.6%
USSR per capita GNP, 1970	$1,997
Same as above, but projecting the net 1958-62 USSR economic growth rate of 3.4 per cent (4.6 per cent economic growth, less 1.2 per cent to allow for growth of population)	
USSR per capita GNP, 1970	$1,618
Same, at net 1960-63 rate of economic growth in Russia of 2.3 per cent (3.5 per cent economic growth rate, less 1.2 per cent population growth)	$1,454
United States per capita GNP, 1962	$3,004

Source: U.S. Congress, Joint Economic Committee, *Annual Economic Indicators for the U.S.S.R.* (1964), pages 3, 5, 95 and 96.

Table 3 · Agriculture in the USSR and the US

I. The US and the USSR Compared

A. Some Key Quantities Item	Unit & Date	USSR	US
Population (July 1)	Mils. 1962	224.8	189.3
Civilian labor force	Mils. 1962	115.0[1]	82.0[2]
Agricultural labor force	Mils. 1962	47.0[3]	7.2[1]
Farm labor force as % of total labor force	Per cent 1962	40.8	8.2
Sown crop land per capita	Acres 1963	2.4	1.6
Tractors on Farms (Jan. 1)	1000s 1963	1,329	5,170
Trucks on Farms	do	875	2,900
Grain Combines	do	520	1,020
Number US Farms	Mils. 1962		3.69
Sown area per farm	Acres 1962		82
Number USSR collectives[4]	1962	39,700	
Sown area per collective[4]	1960	7,010	
Number USSR state farms[4]	1960	8,570	
Sown area per state farm[4]	Acres 1960	24,991	
Sown crop land	Mil. Acres 1963	539	309
Commercial fertilizer used, 1962[5]	Pounds per sown Acre	13	56

II. USSR Investment in Agriculture[6]

Year	(Index) Net USSR Agricultural Output	(Index) USSR Agricultural Investment	(Per Cent) Agricultural Investment As Per Cent Total Investment[6]
1950	100	100	
1951	91	104	
1952	103	104	
1953	104	103	
1954	107	148	
1955	123	204	27.9[9]
1956	139	216	
1957	139	226	
1958	157	255	26.0[9]
1959	148	272	24.4[9]
1960	153[7]	279[9]	22.9[9]
1961	165[7]	307[7]	23.9[9]
1962	157[7]	344[8]	24.8[9]

B. Yields

	USSR as Per Cent of US 1962 — Per Acre
Grain Corn	35%
Wheat	48
Rye	63
Oats	51
Barley	58
Rice	65
Grain Soybean	26
Tobacco	47
Potatoes	33

C. Livestock Production

	USSR as Per cent of US 1962
Beef & Veal	38%
Cow Milk	96
Butter	131
Eggs	48
Wool	149
Poultry Meat	25

Source: U.S. Congress, Joint Economic Committee, *Annual Economic Indicators for the U.S.S.R.* (1964), pp. 29-32, except as noted in footnotes 6 through 9.

[1] Estimate based on U.S.S.R. census, 1959.
[2] Includes all who worked one hour or more during the year.
[3] Includes persons working on their own private plots; based on U.S.S.R. census, 1959.
[4] Does not include private plots (which accounted for 3-4% of sown area, as much larger proportion of livestock, and for about a third of total agricultural production in the U.S.S.R.).
[5] Primary commercial fertilizer in terms of available plant nutrients.
J. E. Willet, in Joint Economic Committee, *Dimensions of Soviet Economic Power* (1962), page 98.
[6] Based on Joint Economic Committee, *Annual Economic Indicators*, as above p. 32.
[8] Based on Joint Economic Committee, *Annual Economic Indicators*, as above, rates of increase for new, fixed, productive agricultural investment, p. 42, Table IV-5.
[9] Derived from Joint Economic Committee, *Annual Economic Indicators*, rates of growth of new, fixed, productive investment, p. 42, Table IV-6.

71

Table 4 · A Comparison of the Growth of Industrial Production, and Productivity, in Russia and the US, 1870-1913 and 1928-1955

Average Annual Growth Rates

	Russia[1]		United States[1]	
	1870/1913	1928/55	1870/1913	1928/55
		Per Cent		
Industrial Growth	5.3%	6.1%[2]	5.1%	3.7%
Output per person engaged in production[4]	[3]	1.6[2]	[3]	1.9
Output per head of population	3.7	5.3	2.9	2.5

Source: G. Warren Nutter, in *Comparisons of the United States and Soviet Economies*, Part I, Page 105 (Joint Economic Committee, U.S. Congress).

Note: See Table 5, and footnotes, for other measurements of Soviet industrial output.

[1] All civilian industrial output.

[2] Adjusted to exclude effects of territorial gains.

[3] Not available.

[4] Full time equivalents.

Table 5
Average Annual Growth of Civilian Industrial Production

Period	USSR	US	Japan	West Germany	France	Italy
			(Per Cent)			
1937-61	5.9	4.3	5.3	4.0[1]	4.0[1]	5.3[1]
1950-55	10.1	5.2	15.5	12.3	5.6	8.8
1955-61	8.7	2.1	18.2	6.6	6.9	9.0
1950-61	9.3	3.5	17.0	9.2	6.4	8.9
1959-62	7.2[2]	4.0[3]				

Source: Rush V. Greenslade and Phyllis Wallace, in *Dimensions of Soviet Economic Power* (Joint Economic Committee, U.S. Congress, 1962), Page 125, except as below.

[1] Initial year 1938.
[2] Joint Economic Committee, *Annual Economic Indicators for the U.S.S.R.*, Tables III–7 & 8.
[3] Federal Reserve Board.

Note on Industrial Indexes: This study cannot include a section on the complexities of constructing a reliable index of Soviet industrial production. It attempts to make use of indexes that appear to have the most general, even if partial acceptance by the principal experts in the field. Through the first four lines, the above table represents a reworking of the Soviet data by Rush V. Greenslade and Phyllis Wallace in *Dimensions of Soviet Economic Power.* The Greenslade-Wallace index improved on others by including more production in its machinery sector than previous similar indexes included, chiefly, the addition of electronics, civil aircraft and shipbuilding.   For the 1950-55 period, a well known earlier index by G. Warren Nutter would indicate industrial growth in the U.S.S.R. of about 10 per cent less than the Greenslade-Wallace index; another well known, but later, index, that of Kaplan-Moorstein, (*Index of Soviet Industrial Output*, Rand Corp. 1960) would indicate about 2.5 per cent less Soviet industrial growth. See *Dimensions*, "Three Indexes of Soviet Civilian Industrial Production, for 1955" (Page 128).

The final figure in Table 5 for U.S.S.R. industrial output, for the period 1959-62, reflects the general slowdown in U.S.S.R. economic growth after 1958. By years, the numbers were 8.6% for 1959, 6.3 for 1960, 6.7 for 1961 and 7.2 for 1962.

It should be noted that the index numbers are for civilian industrial output. In discussing this, Greenslade-Wallace say (*Dimensions*, Page 126) that comparisons of their civilian production index with the studies of Abram Bergson on Soviet national income, including military production, "Strongly suggest that the growth of armaments production from 1937 to 1961 exceeded the growth of civilian industrial production and that the latter is a minimum measure of Soviet industrial growth." This suggests that industrialization for non-military purposes in Soviet Russia could benefit considerably from a reduction of the burden of production for armaments. That is, any increase in the Soviet armaments burden would apparently cut into the growth of industrial production for civilian requirements.

The Greenslade-Wallace index of civilian industrial production in the U.S.S.R. compares as follows with the official Soviet claim to the growth of the gross value of industrial production in the U.S.S.R.: (*Dimensions*, Page 128).

	1950	1951	1952	1953	1954	1955	1956	1957	1958	1959	1960	1961
						(Index, 1955 = 100)						
Official	54	63	70	79	89	100	111	122	134	150	164	179
G-W	61.7	69.0	73.6	80.8	90.3	100	110.7	122.5	133.6	145.0	154.1	164.7

73

Table 6 · The Slowdown of Economic Growth in the USSR, 1950-1963

I. Index, Components of Gross National Product

	1950	1958	1959	Index 1955 = 100 1960	1961	1962	Per Cent Contribution to GNP in 1955
Industry	61.7	133.6	145.0	154.1	164.7	176.5	30.3
Construction	55.6	150.8	173.8	188.9	193.1	197.6	8.8
Agriculture	81.3	126.6	121.5	124.9	135.1	128.4	36.2
Transportation	61.2	137.7	151.7	161.2	171.4	181.8	5.1
Communications	73.6	120.7	129.9	136.8	147.1	157.5	.8
Internal Trade	73.7	115.9	121.0	125.2	130.6	136.3	3.9
Services	88.6	97.6	99.7	103.5	109.5	114.9	14.9
—of which:							
Defense	87.0	70.3	66.7	61.1	61.1	61.1	34.3
Education	83.1	109.8	114.2	120.4	129.5	138.0	28.5
Health	78.1	116.4	123.5	131.7	140.0	145.2	11.8
Gov't. Admin.	134.5	95.1	93.5	91.5	95.2	97.8	9.8
Housing	86.4	116.6	122.4	137.1	145.0	151.3	6.2
Finance	99.6	98.1	98.1	100.0	104.5	106.4	1.9
Science	72.0	134.9	148.6	177.7	198.6	221.2	7.4
Total GNP, Index	72.7	126.5	131.4	138.0	147.0	150.2	100

II. GNP Growth Rates

	1958	1959	1960	1961	1962
a. Annual	9.9%	3.9%	5.0%	6.5%	2.2%

b. Averages, for periods	Aggregate GNP	Per Capita GNP
1950-58	6.8%	5.0%
1958-62	4.6	2.8
1960-63	3.5	—

Source: U.S. Congress, Joint Economic Committee, *Annual Economic Indicators for the U.S.S.R.*, pages 93-98.

Table 7 · A Statistical Profile of the Communist World, 1961

Unit of Measurement	Area (1,000 square miles)	Population (millions)	Gross Natl. Product (billions dollars[3])	Grain[1] Crops (thousand metric tons)	Electric Energy (billion kwh)	Crude Petroleum (thousand metric tons)	Crude Steel (thousand metric tons)	Yarn[2] (thousand metric tons)	Housing (persons per room)
The Russian-Led Bloc:									
Bulgaria	42.7	7.9		3,494	5.4	207	340	65.4	1.8[9]
Czechoslovakia	49.4	13.8		2,127	27.0	150	7,043	166.1	1.5[10]
East Germany	41.7	16.1		1,038	42.5	na	3,444	141.0	na
Hungary	35.9	10.0	100	4,689	8.4	1,457	2,053	73.0	1.4[7]
Mongolia	592.7	.9		126	.1	356	na	na	na
Poland	120.4	30.0		2,825	32.3	203	7,234	248.3	1.7[7]
Rumania	92.0	18.6		9,761	8.7	11,582	2,126	84.5	na
USSR	8,649.5	218.0	253	90,506	327.6	166,068	70,700	1,519.2	1.5[9]
Total	9,624.3	315.3	353[5]	114,566	452.0	179,702[5]	92,941[5]	2,297.5[5]	—
The China-Led Bloc:									
Albania	11.1	1.7	na	252	.2	648	na	na	na
Mainland China	3,691.5	646.5	80	137,734	58.5[7]	5,500[7]	15,000	1,637.6[7]	na
North Korea	47.3	8.4	3	4,830	10.4	na	780	na	na
North Vietnam	61.4	16.7		4,970	.3	na	na	na	na
Total	3,811.3	673.3	83[5]	147,786	69.4	6,148[5]	15,780[5]	1,637.6[5]	—
Yugoslavia	98.8	18.6	5.6	7,744	9.9	1,341	1,532	78.2	2.3[11]
Cuba	44.2	6.9	2.6	582	2.8[6]	10	na	na	3.2[11]
The Communist World	13,578.6	1,014.1	444[5]	270,678	534.1	187,201[5]	110,252[5]	4,013.3[5]	—
The United States	3,615.2[4]	187.0	555	128,097	878.5	354,303	88,917	2,240.0[8]	0.77
World	52,224.7	3,069.0	na	692,100	2,453.3	1,123,700	354,800	na	na

Sources: U.N., *Statistical Yearbook*, 1962 (except, Gross National Products)
Tables: 1, 15, 17, 20, 43, 83, 86, 88, 109, 125, 176
Gross National Products: U.S. Congress, Joint Economic Committee. Annual Economic Indicators for the USSR, 1964, p. 131.

[1]Wheat, corn and rice; [2]Cotton, wool, rayon and acetate; [3]Latest data converted at official exchange rates; [4]Includes Alaska and Hawaii; [5]Derived by addition of available country totals, as above; [6]1959; [7]1960; [8]1958; [9]1956; [10]1950; [11]1953.

Table 8 · Production in the Communist World 1959-1962 (billions of dollars)

Country or Area	1959	1960	1961	1962	Per Cent Growth 1959-62
		GROSS NATIONAL PRODUCT			
USSR	$214	$231	$240	$253	18.2%
Other European Bloc[2]	85	91	96	100	17.6
European Bloc	299	322	336	353	18.1
Mainland China	82	88	79	80	-2.4
Other Asian Bloc[3]	3	3	3	3	—
Asian Bloc	85	91	82	83	-2.4
Sino-Soviet Bloc[4]	384	413	418	436	13.5
Yugoslavia[5]				5.6	
Cuba[5]				2.6	
Communist World				444.2	

Source: U.S. Congress, Joint Economic Committee, *Annual Economic Indicators for the U.S.S.R.* (1964), page 131.

[1] At market prices, converted to purchasing power equivalents.
[2] Includes: Albania, Bulgaria, Czechoslovakia, East Germany, Hungary, Poland and Rumania.
[3] Includes: Mongolia, North Korea and North Vietnam.
[4] Does not include Yugoslavia and Cuba.
[5] Not available on same basis as other countries, 1959-1961.

Table 9 · Red China's Production Targets, Production Claims and Estimated Real Production, 1957-1962

(millions of metric tons)

	1957	1958	1959	1960	1961	1962
Steel						
Plan target	na	8.20	18.00	18.00	na	na
Initial Production Claim	na	10.73	na	na	na	na
Final Production Claim	5.35	8.00	13.25	18.40	na	na
Estimated Real Production[1]	5.00	8.00	10.00	15.00	12.00	10.00[3]
Coal						
Plan target	na	270.0	380.0	425.0	na	na
Initial Production Claim	na	270.0	na	na	na	na
Final Production Claim	124.2	270.0	347.8	na	na	na
Estimated Real Production[1]	100.0	200.0	300.0[3]	400.0[3]	300[3]	240[3]
Grain[2]						
Plan target	na	370	525	300	na	na
Initial Production Claim	na	375	na	na	na	na
Final Production Claim	185	250	270	na	na	na
Estimated Real Production[1]	185	200	180	155	165	182.5
Cotton						
Plan target	na	3.00	5.00	2.65	na	na
Initial Production Claim	na	3.00	na	na	na	na
Final Production Claim	1.65	2.10	2.40	na	na	na
Estimated Real Production[1]	1.65	1.90	1.81	1.55	1.45	1.56

Source: *New York Times*, May 4, 1963.

[1] Estimated by specialists on the Chinese economy in Hong Kong.
[2] Not specified.
[3] Estimated to be less than this amount.
na—Not available.

Table 10
Soviet-Chinese Trade 1950-1962

Year	USSR Exports to China	USSR Imports from China	China's Balance in Resources Exchanged[1]
		(millions of current US dollars)	
1950	$388	$ 188	+ $ 200
1951	476	332	+ 144
1952	554	414	+ 140
1953	698	475	+ 223
1954	759	578	+ 181
1955	748	644	+ 104
1950/55			+ $ 992
1956	733	764	− 31
1957	544	738	− 194
1958	634	881	− 247
1959	935	1,100	− 145
1960	817	848	− 31
1961	367	551	− 184
1962	233	516	− 283
1956/1962			−$1,115

[1] Plus signs for net receipt of resources (a Chinese import surplus); minus signs for net Chinese loss of resources (a Chinese export surplus).

Sources: 1950-1961, U.S. Congress, Joint Economic Committee—*Dimensions of Soviet Economic Power* (1962), page 430; 1959-1962, *Annual Economic Indicators for the U.S.S.R.* (1964), pages 136-137.

Table 11 · Official Claims and Plans:
Production Growth in Comecon Countries, 1950-1980[1] (per cent)

	1950-1961	1960-1980 Plans	
	Industrial Output	Industry	Agriculture
All Comecon Countries	11.5%		
USSR		9.6/9.7%	6.5%
Poland		8.4	3.2
East Germany		7.0	2.3/3.0
Czechoslovakia		8.6	3.4
Hungary		9.0	4.3
Rumania		10.6	5.7/5.8
Bulgaria		10.5	4.2

Source: *International Affairs* (Moscow)
        No. 9, September, 1963
[1] Except Mongolia

Table 12 · Comparison of the Production and Trade of the Eastern European Comecon Nations with the USSR, Western Europe and the US, 1958

Item	Unit of Measurement	Eastern[a] Europe	USSR	USSR as per cent of E. Europe	European Economic Community	EEC as per cent of E. Europe	US[f]
Population	Million persons	95.1*	207.1		165.4*		
Production							
Crude Steel	Tons per 1000 persons	179	265	148.0%	350	195.5%	444
Coal	Tons per 1000 persons	2,482	2,052*	82.5	1,686	67.6	2,193
Crude Oil	Tons per 1000 persons	134*	546	497.5	54	40.3	1,900
Cotton Fabrics[b]	Tons per 1000 persons	2.25	3.28	145.8	5	222.0	7
Five main grains[d]	Tons per 1000 persons	443	599	135.2	288	65.0	857
Electric Power	MWh per 1000 persons	989	1,125	113.8	1,371	139.0	4,152
Motor Vehicles	Vehicles per 1000 pns.	1.57	2.47	163.6	18	1,150.0	29
Leather Shoes	Prs. per 1000 persons	1,409[c]	1,719[c]	122.1	1,451[b]	103.0	3,038
External Trade							
Exports	Dollars per 1000 persons	$62,480	$42,010[e]	34.4%	$137,000	220.0%	$101,803
Imports	Dollars per 1000 persons	59,580			138,500	232.0	73,837

Source: Derived from *Economic Bulletin for Europe* (United Nations Economic Commission for Europe, Geneva, 1959) Vol. 11, No. 1, 1959, Table 13, p. 66.

* Based on estimates by the Secretariat, Economic Commission for Europe.
a Excludes Albania and Yugoslavia.
b 1957.
c Includes small amount of other shoes.
d 1956-58 average.
e Exports and imports.
f A recession year.

Table 13 · The Composition of USSR Foreign Trade, 1955-62

Trade Areas and Selected Trade Items	USSR EXPORTS Per Cent 1955	1958	1961	1962	Million Dollars 1962	USSR IMPORTS Per Cent 1955	1958	1961	1962	Million Dollars 1962
TOTAL TRADE	100	100	100	100	$7,034.7	100	100	100	100	$6,449.7
Machinery & equipment	17.5	18.5	16.1	16.6	1,168.6	30.2	24.5	29.8	34.7	2,239.8
(Transport equipment)	—	—	—	—	—	(12.5)	(9.8)	(9.2)	(11.6)	(745.8)
Petroleum & products	6.7	10.0	12.6	11.5	807.8	4.0	3.1	2.1	1.6	103.0
Rolled ferrous metals	5.6	7.7	8.0	7.7	540.3	.5	2.9	2.8	3.0	192.7
Nonferrous metals	3.2	4.6	3.5	3.1	217.5	4.3	3.1	2.5	2.1	136.4
Chemicals	2.1	2.6	2.9	2.5	176.9	1.7	2.3	2.4	3.3	212.0
Wood & products	5.1	5.6	6.0	6.0	420.4	3.0	2.4	2.1	1.8	118.5
Consumer goods	14.5	15.5	16.8	15.8	1,112.5	21.6	26.7	30.6	28.3	1,822.6
(Food)	(11.2)	(11.8)	(13.2)	(12.8)	(899.0)	(16.9)	(12.9)	(13.3)	(11.1)	(712.8)
(Grain)	(8.3)	(8.3)	(7.9)	(7.5)	(529.4)					
TOTAL, this group	54.7	64.5	65.9	63.2	$4,444.0	65.3	65.0	72.3	74.8	$4,825.0
With East Europe	100	100	100	100	$3,971.2	100	100	100	100	$3,587.5
Machinery & equipment	17.0	10.7	13.2	15.3	606.6	44.1	39.1	40.9	45.2	1,621.5
Unspecified trade [1]	19.0	12.1	14.4	13.9	552.3	8.2	13.3	9.2	9.0	323.5
Petroleum & products	3.1	6.3	8.2	8.3	328.4	6.8	5.3	3.3	2.5	90.2
Rolled ferrous metals	5.4	10.3	11.0	10.6	423.3	.3	.5	1.2	1.2	41.6
Consumer goods	15.9	18.3	14.9	16.2	643.5	11.2	20.2	26.2	24.7	885.9
(Food)	(14.6)	(15.1)	(12.5)	(13.9)	(552.0)	(6.7)	(5.6)	(8.2)	(6.1)	(218.0)
(Grain)	(12.9)	(11.6)	(8.1)	(8.8)	(347.5)					
TOTAL, this group	60.4	57.7	61.7	64.3	$2,553.1	70.6	78.4	80.8	82.6	$2,962.7
With Communist China	100	100	100	100	$ 233.4	100	100	100	100	$ 516.3
Machinery & equipment	30.7	50.2	29.4	11.7	27.3	1.6	.5	—	1.7	8.7
Unspecified trade	43.1	19.1	5.2	19.4	45.2	—	.5	5.5	.7	3.6
Petroleum & products	10.6	14.6	32.9	34.5	80.5					
Rolled ferrous metals	7.2	5.8	5.3	7.7	17.9					
Nonferrous metals						8.7	5.5	6.2	5.0	25.9
(Tin)						(7.4)	(4.5)	(4.1)	(3.4)	(17.5)
Ores & concentrates						9.7	8.4	8.8	6.8	35.3
Consumer goods	.8	1.5	18.4	13.3	31.0	38.1	54.6	65.5	74.0	382.3
(Food)	(.1)	(.2)	(17.4)	(8.9)	(20.8)	(28.5)	(26.1)	(3.2)	(7.4)	(38.1)
TOTAL, this group	92.1	91.2	91.2	86.4	$ 201.9	58.1	69.5	86.0	88.2	$ 455.8
With the Industrialized Free World	100	100	100	100	$1,105.1	100	100	100	100	$1,264.6
Machinery & equipment						42.1	31.2	43.2	47.1	596.0
(Chemical equipment)						(—)	(3.1)	(12.1)	(7.0)	(88.0)
(Transport equipment)						(23.5)	(12.3)	(6.1)	(11.8)	(149.9)
Base metals & manufactures	9.6	14.2	11.2	10.7	118.8	12.4	26.0	22.2	23.3	294.9
(Rolled ferrous metals)	(1.5)	(1.5)	(2.3)	(2.2)	(24.0)	(1.9)	(15.7)	(8.9)	(8.7)	(109.9)
(Pig iron)	(4.6)	(1.9)	(3.8)	(4.2)	(46.0)					
(Tin)	(—)	(4.8)	(.2)	(—)	(—)					
(Pipes)						(.3)	(.2)	(7.4)	(9.5)	(119.6)
Wood & products	20.7	18.4	16.7	18.2	200.9	11.4	10.2	6.4	5.1	64.5
Petroleum & products	8.3	13.5	20.2	22.0	243.3	—	—	—	—	—
Consumer goods	19.8	18.4	19.6	16.6	183.8	10.0	11.5	6.8	4.7	59.2
(Food)	(12.9)	(12.7)	(14.9)	(11.8)	(103.1)					
(Grain)	(8.8)	(9.4)	(12.1)	(8.4)	(93.2)					
(Furs & pelts)	(6.6)	(5.1)	(3.9)	(4.2)	(46.2)					
Textile materials	12.0	5.9	4.9	4.8	52.6	6.9	8.1	7.7	6.1	77.3
TOTAL, this group	70.4	70.4	72.6	72.3	$ 798.8	82.8	87.0	86.3	86.3	$1,091.9
With the Underdeveloped Free World	100	100	100	100	$ 567.7	100	100	100	100	$ 614.0
Machinery & equipment	4.8	41.2	46.5	50.4	285.9					
(Complete plants)	(1.0)	(28.8)	(27.4)	(32.6)	(184.9)					
Petroleum & products	28.4	20.1	13.3	11.0	62.2					
Rolled ferrous metals	14.4	8.6	4.6	5.6	31.7					
Nonferrous metals						.1	—	3.4	3.3	20.4
Food	9.4	11.7	9.4	12.1	68.7	45.6	19.1	16.9	22.8	140.3
Wood & products	13.6	7.8	7.5	6.0	34.0					
Cotton						9.0	28.1	20.9	18.2	112.0
Natural Rubber						12.1	27.3	38.5	33.5	205.9
TOTAL, this group	70.6	89.4	81.3	85.1	$ 482.5	66.8	74.5	79.7	77.8	$ 478.6

Source: U.S. Congress, Joint Economic Committee, *Annual Economic Indicators for the U.S.S.R.* (1964), pp. 105-113.

[1] Indicative of the magnitude of military-strategic trade of the U.S.S.R. within the bloc.
—=Not a principal trade item (blanks indicate no trade, or negligible trade).
( )=Detail of preceding trade class; per cents show portion of all trade under the geographical division.

Table 14 · Main Trading Partners in Soviet Trade in Machinery & Equipment, 1961 (per cent of total)

Trade Partner	USSR Imports 100%	USSR Exports 100%
European Bloc	71.6	47.6
(East Germany)	(28.4)	(5.9)
(Czechoslovakia)	(19.3)	(8.6)
Free World Developed	27.3	
(West Germany)	(5.2)	
Asian Bloc		19.2
(Communist China)		(11.2)
Free World Underdeveloped		31.2
(Cuba)		(6.3)
(India)		(5.6)
(UAR)		(4.6)

Source: *Dimensions of Soviet Economic Power*, Joint Economic Committee, U.S. Congress, 1962, p. 449.

Table 15 · USSR, US and World Trade 1950 and 1955-1962 (Millions of current US dollars)

	Total USSR Foreign Trade	USSR TRADE WITH COMMUNIST COUNTRIES					USSR TRADE WITH FREE WORLD				Total[3] US Foreign Trade	Total World Trade (% USSR)
		Total	East Europe	Mainland China	Other Asian	Other[1]	Total	Industrial Countries	Underdeveloped[2] Countries	Other		
1950 TOTALS	$ 3,250	$2,637	$1,866	$ 576	$ 195	—	$ 613	n.a.	n.a.	n.a.	$18,885	$113,700 (2.8%)
1955 Totals	6,488	4,141	3,465	1,492	261	33	1,346	975	322	49	26,756	191,000 (3.4%)
Exports	3,427	2,823	1,792	748	166	16	704	544	112	48	15,419	
Imports	3,061	2,418	1,663	644	95	17	642	431	210	1	11,337	
Balance	+366	+305	+129	+104	+71	−1	+62	+113	−98	+47	+4,082	
1956 Totals	7,228	5,465	3,583	1,497	267	119	1,763	1,176	477	111	31,456	211,200 (3.4%)
Exports	3,615	2,729	1,768	733	160	69	886	597	180	109	18,940	
Imports	3,613	2,736	1,815	764	107	50	877	579	297	2	12,516	
Balance	+ 2	− 7	− 47	− 31	+ 53	+ 19	+ 9	+ 18	−117	+107	+6,424	
1957 Totals	8,319	6,131	4,465	1,282	253	130	2,189	1,363	718	108	33,622	230,000 (3.6%)
Exports	4,381	3,305	2,550	544	137	73	1,077	690	283	104	20,671	
Imports	3,938	2,826	1,915	738	116	57	1,112	673	435	4	12,951	
Balance	+343	+479	+635	−194	+ 21	+ 16	− 35	+ 17	−152	+100	+7,720	
1958 Totals	8,648	6,378	4,526	1,515	235	102	2,268	1,292	861	106	30,484	220,400 (3.9%)
Exports	4,298	3,136	2,320	634	131	51	1,161	670	389	102	17,745	
Imports	4,350	3,242	2,206	881	104	51	1,108	622	482	4	12,739	
Balance	− 52	−106	+114	−247	+ 27	—	+ 53	+ 48	− 93	+ 98	+5,006	
1959 Totals	10,514	7,914	5,470	2,054	290	99	2,601	1,613	866	123	34,876	235,900 (4.4%)
Exports	5,441	4,124	2,951	954	173	46	1,317	856	344	118	17,438	
Imports	5,073	3,790	2,519	1,100	117	53	1,284	757	522	5	14,994	
Balance	+368	+334	+432	−146	+ 56	−7	+ 33	+ 99	−178	+113	+2,444	
1960 Totals	11,191	8,187	5,937	1,665	301	283	3,004	2,042	921	43	34,999	262,500 (4.3%)
Exports	5,562	4,208	3,118	817	147	126	1,354	972	346	37	20,349	
Imports	5,629	3,979	2,819	848	154	157	1,650	1,070	575	6	14,650	
Balance	− 67	+229	+299	− 31	− 7	− 31	−296	− 98	−229	+ 31	+5,599	
1961 Totals	11,825	8,457	6,444	918	374	720	3,369	2,148	1,091	130	35,374	273,600 (4.3%)
Exports	5,998	4,310	3,400	367	211	332	1,688	1,060	507	121	20,717	
Imports	5,827	4,147	3,044	551	163	388	1,681	1,088	584	9	14,657	
Balance	+171	+163	+356	−184	+ 48	− 56	+ 7	− 28	− 77	+112	+6,060	
1962 Totals	13,485	9,472	7,559	749	441	723	4,012	2,370	1,182	462	37,608	288,420[4] (4.8%)
Exports	7,035	4,909	3,971	233	262	443	2,125	1,105	568	453	21,359	
Imports	6,450	4,563	3,588	516	179	280	1,887	1,265	614	9	16,249	
Balance	+585	+346	+383	−283	+ 83	+163	+238	−160	− 46	+444	+5,110	

Sources: U.S. Congress, Joint Economic Committee, *Annual Economic Indicators for the U.S.S.R.* (1964), p. 104; except: United Nations, *Statistical Yearbook 1962* and OECD, *General Statistics*, March, 1964 for world trade; U.S. Department of Commerce, *Statistical Abstracts of the United States*, 1961 and 1963, and *Survey of Current Business*, March, 1964, for U.S. trade.

[1] Includes, after 1955, Yugoslavia; 1960 and after, Cuba; 1961 and after, Albania (which before 1961 is included in East Europe).
[2] Before 1960, includes Cuba.
[3] Includes U.S. economic and military aid shipments, and special category exports.
[4] Trade of communist countries partly estimated.

Table 16 · Trends in USSR Trade with Free World Countries and Communist Countries, 1955-1962 (millions of dollars)

USSR Trade[1] with	1955	1956	1957	1958	1959	1960	1961	1962	Per Cent Changes 1955/58	Per Cent Changes 1958/62
FREE WORLD, Total[2]	$ 1,346	$ 1,763	$ 2,189	$ 2,269	$ 2,601	$ 3,005	$ 3,369	$ 4,012	+ 68.5	+ 76.8
Industrial Countries including:	$ 974	$ 1,176	$ 1,363	$ 1,292	$ 1,612	$ 2,041	$ 2,148	$ 2,370	+ 32.6	+ 83.4
Finland	234	261	316	254	287	293	279	396	+ 8.5	+ 9.8
United Kingdom	240	223	289	219	257	301	355	330	− 9.8	+ 62.1
West Germany	53	110	133	138	209	318	298	339	+ 160.3	+ 145.6
France	96	120	115	168	188	204	200	238	+ 75.0	+ 41.6
Italy	34	60	75	74	131	193	226	230	+ 117.6	+ 205.4
Sweden	46	61	57	58	86	100	103	130	+ 26.0	+ 77.5
Belgium	39	61	59	39	37	51	68	79	n.a.	+ 102.5
Netherlands	66	52	66	75	80	70	76	90	+ 13.6	+ 20.0
United States	24	32	26	31	44	85	75	44	+ 29.1	+ 41.9
Underdeveloped Countries including:	$ 323	$ 476	$ 718	$ 871	$ 866	$ 920	$ 1,091	$ 1,182	+ 169.6	+ 25.2
Egypt	26	89	193	195	181	191	205	176	+ 650.0	− 9.8
India	12	59	127	181	129	116	162	196	+ 1,408.3	+ 8.2
Malaya	22	84	49	118	128	114	172	163	+ 436.3	+ 38.1
Afghanistan	25	33	39	36	44	49	59	65	+ 44.0	+ 80.5
Argentina	52	32	26	33	45	36	30	18	− 36.6	− 55.5
Iran	42	34	50	54	37	37	36	33	+ 28.5	− 48.9
Indonesia	4	13	36	39	27	48	65	97	+ 875.0	+ 148.7
Other Free World Countries	$ 49	$ 111	$ 108	$ 106	$ 123	$ 43	$ 130	$ 461	+ 116.3	+ 22.6
COMMUNIST WORLD, Total[3]	$ 4,141	$ 5,465	$ 6,131	$ 6,378	$ 7,914	$ 8,187	$ 8,457	$ 9,472	+ 54.0	+ 48.5
East Europe Satellites[4]	$ 3,465	$ 3,583	$ 4,465	$ 4,526	$ 5,470	$ 5,937	$ 6,444	$ 7,559	+ 30.6	+ 67.0
Underdeveloped Communist Countries[5]	$ 676	$ 1,882	$ 1,666	$ 1,852	$ 2,444	$ 2,250	$ 2,013	$ 1,913	+ 173.9	+ 3.2
TOTAL USSR TRADE	$ 5,487	$ 7,228	$ 8,320	$ 8,647	$10,515	$11,192	$11,826	$13,484	+ 57.5	+ 55.9
Per cent of USSR Trade with										
Industrial Free World	17.7%	16.2	16.3	14.9	15.3	18.2	18.1	17.5	− 15.9	+ 17.4
Other Free World	7.6%	8.1	9.9	11.2	9.4	8.6	10.3	12.1	+ 47.3	+ 8.0
Total Free World	25.3%	24.3	26.2	26.1	24.7	26.8	28.4	29.6	+ 3.1	+ 13.4

Source: U.S. Congress, Joint Economic Committee, *Annual Economic Indicators for the U.S.S.R.* (1964), pages 104 and 114.

[1] Exports plus imports.
[2] Before 1960, includes Cuba; 1960 and after, Cuba included among underdeveloped Communist countries.
[3] Includes Yugoslavia and, 1960 and after, Cuba.
[4] Representing Russia's industrialized trade partners of the Communist world. Includes Albania through 1960.
[5] Includes Yugoslavia in addition to Red China, Mongolia, North Korea, North Vietnam and, after 1960, Albania; after 1959, includes Cuba.

Table 17 · Sino-Soviet Bloc, USSR and US Economic Aid Commitments, 1945-1963 (millions of dollars)

Donors / Recipients	SINO-SOVIET BLOC	Credits (1954-1962[2])	Grants (1954-1962[2])	USSR 1945-62[1]	USSR 1954-62[1]	USSR 1963	UNITED STATES 1945-62[1]	UNITED STATES 1954-62[1]	UNITED STATES 1963
	Total								
FREE WORLD TOTAL*	$4,336	$4,180	$236	$3,227	$3,227	$168	$64,188	$29,286	$5,025
Latin America	$ 110	$ 110	0	$ 100	$ 100	—	$ 5,867	$ 4,591	$ 929
Argentina	104	104	0	100	100	—	572	470	153
Bolivia	2	2	0	—	—	—	258	233	68
Brazil	4	4	0	—	—	—	1,737	1,170	145
Middle East	$1,647	$1,561	$ 86	$1,425	$1,425	$ 45	$ 4,607	$ 3,814	$ 581
Afghanistan	515	435	80	507	507	—	217	193	17
Iran	6	6	0	39	39	—	732	657	56
Iraq	216	216	0	183	183	1	22	18	1
Syria	178	178	0	151	151	—	96	95	−13
Turkey	17	17	0	10	10	—	1,580	1,251	178
Egypt	671	666	5	509	509	44	608	576	200
Yemen	44	43	1	26	26	—	23	23	6
Africa	$ 678	$ 644	$ 14	$ 433	$ 433	$101	$ 1,717	$ 1,663	$ 496
Algeria	114	112	2	102	102	101	15	15	80
Ethiopia	200	200	0	95	95	—	118	111	15
Ghana	125	119	6	71	71	—	156	156	3
Guinea	100	100	0	55	55	—	13	13	16
Mali	5	5	0	—	—	—	5	5	4
Morocco	63	57	6	57	57	—	352	352	74
Somali Rep.	25	25	0	—	—	—	28	28	8
Sudan	25	25	0	25	25	—	65	65	10
Tunisia	46	46	0	28	28	—	293	293	64
Asia	$1,895	$1,759	$136	$1,266	$1,266	$ 22	$19,534	$13,602	$2,090
Burma	93	93	0	7	7	7	93	65	24
Cambodia	65	8	57	6	6	—	251	251	19
Ceylon	58	42	16	30	30	15	79	79	5
India	950	946	4	811	811	—	3,867	3,533	835
Indonesia	641	640	1	369	369	—	682	393	122
Nepal	55	0	55	10	10	—	48	48	19
Pakistan	33	30	3	33	33	—	1,854	1,733	362
Europe	$ 6	$ 1	0	—	$ 3	—	$27,756	$ 3,042	$ 351
Cyprus	1	1	0	—	—	—	17	17	11
Iceland	5	5	0	—	3	—	71	36	1
Not Allocated by Country							$ 4,707	$ 2,574	$ 578
COMMUNIST COUNTRIES	$ 548	$ 548	0	$6,594	$2,324	[6]	$ 2,267	$ 1,150	$ 121
Cuba	437	437	0	300	300	[6]	41	29	—
Yugoslavia	111[2]	111[2]	0	73	73	—	1,703	1,040	113
Bloc Countries				6,221[4]	1,951[5]	[6]	523	81	8
GRAND TOTALS	$4,884	$4,728	$156	$9,821	$5,551	$168	$66,455	$30,436	$5,146

Sources: Sino-Soviet Bloc: Department of State, Research Memorandum RSB-145 (September 18, 1962); *The Sino-Soviet Economic Offensive through June 30, 1962,* p. 9. U.S.S.R., 1945-1962: U.S. Congress, Joint Economic Committee, G. S. Carnett and M. H. Crawford in *Dimensions of Soviet Economic Power,* p. 474, except 1963, Joint Economic Committee, *An-nual Economic Indicators for the U.S.S.R.,* p. 117; United States, 1945-1962: Agency for International Development, *U.S. Foreign Assistance, July 1, 1945-June 30, 1962* (Revised) (April 24, 1963); 1963, U.S. Dept. of State, *Proposed Mutual Defense and Development Programs, FY 1965.*

*Note: Countries are those included in Bloc aid. U.S. overall, and regional totals include aid to all countries but exclude $5.2 billion U.S. investment in five international institutions.

[1] June 30, 1962.
[2] Excludes $353 million of expired credits.
[3] Preliminary.
[4] Includes, millions of dollars credits: Albania, $246; Bulgaria, $569; Czechoslovakia, $62; East Germany, $1,353; Hungary, $381; Poland, $914; Rumania, $189; Communist China, $790; North Korea, $690; North Vietnam, $369; Outer Mongolia, $658.
[5] Includes, millions of dollars credits: Albania, $93 (1959); East Germany, $947 (including $310 in 1962 which may partly duplicate earlier credits) (1960, 1961 and 1962); Communist China, $360 (1961); North Vietnam, $229 (1959, 1960 and 1961); Outer Mongolia, $321 (1960 and 1961).
[6] New credits probably extended in 1963 but amounts not available.

Table 18 · Trade Balances of the Sino-Soviet Bloc with Underdeveloped Countries, 1954-1962 (millions of dollars)

TRADE OF		AFRICA 1954-59	AFRICA 1960-62	AFRICA 1954-62	NEAR EAST 1954-59	NEAR EAST 1960-62	NEAR EAST 1954-62	FAR EAST[1] 1954-59	FAR EAST[1] 1960-62	FAR EAST[1] 1954-62	LATIN AMERICA 1954-59	LATIN AMERICA 1960-62	LATIN AMERICA 1954-62	NET TOTAL 1954-62[3]
Total Sino-Soviet Bloc[2][3]	Imports (+)		+309.2			+879.3			+1,220.1			+597.3		
	Exports (−)		−387.3			−957.7			−1,464.3			−416.1		
	Net	$ −126.4	− 78.1	−200.7	+147.8	− 78.4	+ 69.4	− 733.4	− 244.2	− 977.6	+161.7	+181.2	+342.9	−935.73
East Europe	Imports (+)		+145.3			+461.7			+388.9			+321.9		
	Exports (−)		−241.9			−520.7			−354.1			−297.5		
	Net	$ − 99.9	− 96.6	−196.5	+ .2	− 59.0	− 58.8	+ 34.7	+ 34.8	+ 69.5	+ 7.4	+ 24.4	+ 31.8	− 154.0
USSR	Imports (+)		+118.6			+327.4			+596.7			+134.9		
	Exports (−)		− 88.1			−368.0			−390.1			−115.1		
	Net	$+ 82.4	+ 30.5	+112.9	+ 42.1	− 40.6	+ 1.5	+ 270.0	+ 206.6	+ 476.6	+127.0	+ 19.8	+146.8	+ 737.8
European Bloc	Imports (+)		+263.9			+789.1			+985.6			+456.8		
	Exports (−)		−330.0			−888.7			−744.2			−412.6		
	Net	$ − 17.5	− 66.1	− 83.6	+ 42.3	− 99.6	− 57.3	+ 304.7	+ 241.4	+ 546.1	+134.4	+ 44.2	+178.6	+ 583.8
Communist China[4]	Imports (+)		+ 45.3 (1960-61)			+ 90.2 (1960-61)			+ 234.5 (1960-61)			+140.5 (1960-61)	(1954-61)	
	Exports (−)		− 57.3			− 69.0			− 720.1			− 3.5		
	Net	$ −105.1	− 12.0	−117.1 (1954-61)	+105.5	+ 21.2	+126.7 (1954-61)	−1,088.1	− 485.6	−1,523.7 (1954-61)	+ 27.3	+137.0	+164.3	−1,519.53

Source: 1945-59 U.S. Department of Commerce; 1960-61, U.S. Department of State, *Battle Act Report 1963*, pp. 53/54; 1962, U.S. Congress, Joint Economic Committee, *Annual Economic Indicators for the U.S.S.R.*, p. 119.

[1] Excludes Japan.

[2] Includes Mongolia, North Korea and North Vietnam.

[3] Communist China, and Total Sino-Soviet Bloc include, for 1962, an estimated −$169.7 (Chinese export surplus), which is the average of China's balances for 1960 and 1961.

[4] 1961 last year available.

Table 19 · Total Free World Trade and Free World Trade with the Sino-Soviet Bloc and Components, 1947-61¹ (millions of dollars)

FREE WORLD EXPORTS AND IMPORTS	WORLD	SINO-SOVIET BLOC²	EXPORTS TO BLOC AS PER CENT OF EXPORTS TO WORLD	EUROPEAN BLOC	EAST EUROPE	USSR	EXPORTS TO USSR AS PER CENT OF EXPORTS TO WORLD	COMMUNIST CHINA
EXPORTS TO								
1947	$ 48,567	$ 2,005.7	4.1%	$1,333.5	$ 856.5	$ 477.0	1.0%	$ 672.2
1948	53,784	1,968.5	3.7	1,434.2	900.7	533.5	1.0	534.3
1949	55,131	1,666.7	3.0	1,342.6	914.2	428.4	.8	324.1
1950	57,235	1,544.8	2.7	1,092.7	791.6	301.1	.5	452.1
1951	76,990	1,688.5	2.2	1,242.3	854.8	387.5	.5	446.2
1952	74,170	1,438.2	1.9	1,165.7	682.4	483.3	.7	272.5
1953	75,000	1,388.8	1.9	1,101.4	677.9	423.5	.6	287.4
1954	77,700	1,767.1	2.3	1,472.7	896.0	576.7	.7	294.2
1955	84,600	2,087.9	2.5	1,770.6	1,158.1	612.5	.7	317.3
1956	93,900	2,560.7	2.7	2,126.5	1,327.3	799.2	.9	434.2
1957	100,800	3,118.1	3.1	2,584.1	1,567.2	1,016.9	1.0	527.8
1958	96,200	3,426.3	3.6	2,647.0	1,634.1	1,012.9	1.1	770.9
1959	102,200	3,669.4	3.6	3,001.9	1,852.9	1,149.0	1.1	651.6
1960¹	113,082	4,271.9	3.8	3,619.9	2,162.0	1,457.9	1.3	636.9
1961¹	118,266	4,511.3	3.8	3,837.8	2,313.0	1,524.8	1.3	646.6
IMPORTS FROM								
1947	$ 53,327	$ 1,424.7	2.7%	$1,006.8	$ 732.9	$ 273.9	.5%	$ 417.9
1948	59,935	2,008.0	3.4	1,519.7	1,026.0	493.7	.8	488.3
1949	60,030	1,796.8	3.0	1,370.6	1,089.9	280.7	.5	426.2
1950	59,894	1,727.0	2.9	1,192.3	940.0	252.3	.4	534.7
1951	81,780	1,883.0	2.3	1,358.1	967.5	390.6	.5	524.7
1952	80,570	1,663.9	2.0	1,262.9	794.6	468.3	.6	367.9
1953	76,700	1,631.1	2.1	1,189.7	807.9	381.8	.6	432.7
1954	79,900	1,842.6	2.3	1,455.9	955.5	500.4	.6	379.7
1955	89,400	2,434.9	2.7	1,938.0	1,284.1	653.9	.7	487.1
1956	98,800	2,963.1	3.0	2,305.6	1,473.0	832.6	.8	641.4
1957	108,500	3,209.5	3.0	2,562.1	1,520.2	1,041.9	1.0	624.0
1958	101,600	3,509.8	3.5	2,736.0	1,690.5	1,045.5	1.0	755.8
1959	107,100	3,730.1	3.5	3,011.6	1,774.4	1,237.2	1.2	693.4
1960	118,782⁴	4,353.1	3.7⁴	3,562.8	2,127.3	1,435.5	1.2	766.7
1961	124,066⁴	4,518.9	3.6⁴	3,853.3	2,259.7	1,593.6	1.3	637.5
CUBA'S								
Exports to								
1959		$ 13.9		$ 13.1	$ .2	$ 12.9		$ .1
1960		149.5		115.7	12.2	103.5		32.1
1961		478.9		379.5	70.5	309.0		95.6
Imports from								
1959³		$ 1.3		$ 1.3	$ 1.3	$ —		$ —
1960		89.6		89.6	18.8	70.8		n.a.
1961		389.5		389.5	113.6	275.9		n.a.

Sources: U.S. State Department, *Battle Act Report, 1963*, Tables 3A-3D, except Cuba, 1959, for which U.S. State Department, *The Battle Act in New Times* (1962), Tables 3C & 3D.

¹ Cuba included in Free World through 1959, after 1959 excluded.
² Includes Mongolia, North Korea and North Vietnam.
³ Partly estimated.
⁴ Cuban Imports from world not available, estimated same as exports.
n.a.—Not available.

Table 20 · How Gross National Product is Produced:
Underdeveloped and Industrialized Countries; 1950-59

ORIGIN OF INCOME, PER CENT SHARES

Per Capita Income Groups	Industry				Primary Goods	Services
	Total	Manufac-turing	Construc-tion	Other		
Underdeveloped Countries						
Less than $125 per capita income	19	11	4	5	47	33
$125 to $249	25	14	5	6	40	35
$250 to $374	26	16	5	6	30	45
$375 and more	28	17	5	6	27	46
High Income industrial countries[1]	49	32	6	11	13	37

Source: United Nations, *World Economic Survey*, 1961, Table I-1.

[1] Countries with per capita income over $800—Belgium, Canada, Denmark, West Germany, France, Netherlands, Norway, the United Kingdom and the United States (Sweden excluded for lack of data).

II. Communist Man and His Marxist World

Via Dolorosa:
Socialism to Communism

The Mainspring
of Russian Marxism

If Russia's planners can learn to produce Marxist plenty (perhaps with the tools of market forces) the material basis will be established for the fully communist, abundant society. The way would be open to the eventual, if rather far off, equalling of the United States living standard. Meanwhile, Soviet Russia would enjoy improvements in its living standard of kinds and in quantity that would at last make the long deprived Russian people more or less first class citizens of the 20th Century.

Yet, the creation of a Marxist affluent society would by itself offer the world nothing more than a carbon copy of the West's most brilliant commonplace: a high standard of material well being. However hard Soviet propagandists worked to cover it up, the imitative nature of this triumph would out, unless the West meanwhile permitted its living standard to decay.

But Marxist Russia does not intend to rest its claim to world leadership only upon the material victories it expects to win.

The more dynamic claim of the mature materialistic society is a moralistic assertion: that through "communist consciousness" imbued in a disciplined march from capitalism through socialism to communism, the Marxist society can bring forth "the most just and perfect human society, when all the finest traits of the free man will unfold to the full . . ." as the official presentation of the Seven Year Plan to the CPSU put it.

91

The assertion is a revisiting of Marxism's utopian romance. Nevertheless, it is also a formulation of Marxism's claim to be building the good and just society in the USSR that we cannot afford to ignore, for *it seeks to reverse the roles of the Marxist materialistic, and the capitalist humanistic, societies.*

The New Program of the Russian Communist Party spelled it out in 1961:

> The building of a communist society has become an immediate practical task for the Soviet people. . . .

> What is Communism?

> Communism is a classless social system with one form of public ownership of the means of production and full social equality of all members of society; under it, the all-round development of people will be accompanied by the growth of the productive forces through continuous progress in science and technology, all sources of public wealth will gush forth abundantly, and the great principle, "from each according to his ability, to each according to his needs" will be implemented. . . . Labor for the good of society will become the prime and vital requirement of everyone, a necessity recognized by all. . . .

> A high degree of communist consciousness, industry, discipline and devotion to the public interest are qualities typifying the man of Communist society. . . .

> The social economy reaches the highest stage of planned organization, and the most effective and rational use is made of the material wealth and labor reserves to meet the growing requirements of the members of society.

> Under communism, the classes, and socio-economic and cultural distinctions, and differences in living conditions between town and countryside, disappear completely . . . mental and physical labor will merge. . . .

> Communist society, which is based on highly organized production and advanced technology, alters the character of work, but it does not release the members of society from work. . . . Communist production demands high standards of organization, precision and discipline, which are assured, not by compulsion, but thanks to an understanding of

public duty, and are determined by the whole tenor of life in Communist society. . . .

Communism represents the highest form of organization of public life. . . . All production units and self-governing associations will be harmoniously interlinked by a common planned economy and a uniform rhythm of social labor. . . .

Communism is the system under which the abilities and talents of free man, his best moral qualities, blossom forth and reveal themselves in full. Family relations will be completely freed from material considerations and will be based solely on mutual love and friendship.[1]

It is one of the great visions. Any free world nation possessed of a modern industrial establishment and the will to produce the first fully good life for mankind can do it at least one generation ahead of Soviet Russia, and without coercion of the public. What Marxism adds as its exclusive own objective is the production of a "new man", remotivated toward his society and the world by a "communist consciousness" of public duty. But communist consciousness does not just come about. It is learned, and earned, on a long march, by a stony road, through the scorched lands of destroyed capitalism, to a socialist frontier region of saving and deprivation, where the regeneration is completed in the tilling and building of a great production system.

Communist man is indispensable to a society that will take "from each according to his ability" and give to each "according to his needs." But communist new man is not the only product of this Marxist *via dolorosa* that leads to green pastures. Here is also produced what is indispensable to the Marxist leadership: justification for unbending, unending one-party dictatorship. And there is a further dynamic product — *Russian* Marxist leadership justifies itself as the primate of world communism on the grounds that it is the only leadership that has been along the whole *via dolorosa,* and brought its people near fulfillment. In the remainder of this section of Part II we will examine the "socialism to communism" process—its roots in Marxist "law", its specific tasks, and its leadership payoff — as the mainspring of Russian Marxism.

---

[1] *New York Times,* August 1, 1961.

The Law Governed
March

Marxism asserts that Marx and Lenin identified and disclosed certain "law governed" processes of the past, present and future, processes binding upon the society of man. This "Marxist-Leninist law" is projected to the world as a special writ of economic and political development. Marxism asserts that all nations desirous of "scientific" progress toward a higher stage of human experience must honor the writ.

For his part, Marx analysed the capitalism of his day (middle 19th Century) and worked out a theory as to how and why capitalism must inevitably tear itself apart in the throes of an atavistic contest for command over the earth's riches. But Marx did not get around to drawing up the operating rules for the real life operation of a communist community, or nation, much less, a communist nations system. As the original and chief practitioner of Marxism, Soviet Russia has had to improvise most of the rules of communist life and government for itself.

Lenin made a critical addition to Marxism, in terms of the practical governance of the real communist state, by emphasizing one of the "law governed" processes. He reminded Russians that communism would not result from the destruction of capitalism, that the condition of communism, in fact, would only come about much later, following a long and painful experience in an intermediate stage called socialism.[1]

Lenin wrote:

From capitalism mankind can pass directly only to socialism, i.e., to the social ownership of the means of production and the distribution of products according to the amount of work performed by each individual. Our Party looks farther ahead: socialism must inevitably pass gradually into communism, upon the banner of which is inscribed the

---

[1] In Marxist terminology socialism means only what it means in Lenin's context: pre-communism, a stage of organization of a society on the road to communism. It is "a stage at which, though capitalist 'exploitation' has ceased and counter-revolution has been made impossible through imposing dictatorship of the proletariat, the full programme of Communism cannot be realized" (*The Language of Communism,* Harry Hodgkinson, Pitman Publishing Corp., New York, 1954, published in the United Kingdom as *Doubletalk*).

(footnote continued on next page)

motto: "From each according to his ability, to each according to his needs".[1]

From capitalism the next halt could *only* be socialism. The purgatory of socialism is not just a beneficial thing, in Marxism-Leninism it is mandatory. Lenin said it, so it is "Marxist-Leninist law", and the wandering in the desert is, therefore, "law governed history" that cannot be evaded by any nation desirous of attaining to the "higher stage of human development" represented by true communism. Nor can the journey be swift, for the progress out of socialism into communism, Lenin said, will be "gradual". Here too an important dynamic of political power is involved, for upon the "law" that the transformation must be gradual Lenin's Russian successors in Marxism arrogated to themselves an indefinitely long grant of authority to rule as an advanced, already transformed elite.

The Chinese Marxists learned that by Russian Marxist standards they might wander forever on Sinai's stony slopes, and never receive the Law unto themselves. But the East German, the Rumanian, the Bulgarian, the Hungarian, the Polish and the Mongolian Marxists, being under Russian leadership, have had high hope held out to them that they will not be kept thirsting in the desert overlong. When and if Yugoslavia could enter the promised land was a matter of conjecture and accommodation with Moscow. As for Albania, Red China's Marxist ally in Europe, little hope was felt, as was also the case of North Korea

_____

(Footnote continued from preceding page)

The communist use of socialism is entirely distinct from what is meant by socialism as a separate political-economic philosophy, such as the Democratic Socialist parties of the West. In Western political usage socialism is generally regarded as a political movement which is an end in itself (even though Marxist), not a step on the road to communism. Marx is said to have declared that he was "not a Marxist". He certainly was not a Leninist, and it is from Lenin, not Marx, that the guide lines to real life Marxist communism are derived.

Like communism, socialism (according to the Leninist view) is not seized, but must evolve. The Soviet writer A. I. Pashkov said in *Economic Law Concerning the Faster Growth of Output of Producer's Goods*, (Moscow, 1958, reviewed in *American Economic Review*, September, 1959) that socialism was "established in Russia" no sooner than 1936, the two decades from 1917 to 1936 being the "period of transformation from capitalism to socialism". Chou En-Lai, Premier of Red China, announced September 30, 1963—on the eve of the 14th anniversary of the establishment of Marxism throughout Mainland China—that China had "at last found the key to Socialist construction" (*New York Times,* October 1, 1963).

[1] *Control Figures,* p. 115, citing Lenin's *Works,* Vol. 24, p. 62.

and North Vietnam, unless they should find their way out of China's Marxist radicalism into Russia's Marxist orthodoxy.

The Tasks
of Pre-Communism

Overcome Scarcity

The first feature distinguishing socialism from the higher stage of communism is scarcity of material and cultural goods and services. This means that in the condition of socialism, goods and services must be rationed. The rationing is accomplished by parceling things out "according to work", which is to say, according to how much money (or equivalents of money, such as political pull) one's energies, talents and loyalty to the Marxist Establishment can secure.[1] Individuals with greater energies, more talents, and greater political know-how will receive more than those with lesser endowments (or, those worse positioned to use their endowments, such as a peasant in a back village). In socialism, therefore, there are the rich and the poor, the educated and the ignorant, the privileged and the deprived, and *the society's progress in achieving its goals depends upon the effectiveness with which the familiar capitalistic money incentive is used by the Marxist state struggling to achieve communism.*

What this means, outside Marxist terminology, is that under socialism things continue up to a point much as in capitalism: you work, you get paid for your work, and you buy what your pay permits. But the similarity to free enterprise is severely limited and controlled by several underlying dissimilarities: (1) the state owns most things, and therefore nearly all profits of economic enterprise go to the state, and (2) the state is the monopoly supplier to the monopoly producer, so it sets nearly all prices of goods and services, and (3) the state is the monopoly employer, so it sets wage rates.

Under these conditions, rationing "according to work" can

---

[1] For an amusing exploration of the importance of political pull in terms of money equivalents, see the novel, *The Banker's Daughter,* by Vladimir B. Grinioff, Pyramid Books, New York, 1959.

be used by the Marxist state (1) to squeeze the maximum profits out of its people (by paying low wages and low prices for farm goods, and charging high prices at retail); (2) to give high incentives where high effort is most wanted (apartments, cars and high pay to engineers, scientists, entertainers, and Party officials); (3) to keep consumption down (by producing only as much of consumption goods and services as the state wants to produce, and by charging high retail prices); and (4) to keep investment high (by using the high profits resulting from low wages, low farm prices, and high retail prices as savings to finance more production of capital).

The period of "building socialism", therefore, is used to overcome scarcity *in the way that best serves the Marxist managers of the society*. The primary objective is not that of overcoming the *people's* poverty, but is that of overcoming the *state's* poverty. The immediate aims are to enrich and strengthen the state, in terms of endowing it with an advanced production system and an advanced military establishment. While this is being done the people are forced to remain poor.[1] Our survey of the USSR economy in Part I shows the process at work.

But there is an eventual end to the benefits to the state and the Party to be had from the crudities, cruelties and frustrations of the "building socialism" period. Two converging forces signal the end. First, there is some vanishing point to the patience and endurance of even the most docile people, even people such as the Russians who have never known freedom and seem to have little hankering for it.[2] A feeling grows among them that they have earned some rewards, and that a beginning should be made on

---

[1] Wherever it occurs, the process of investment requires giving up something in the present to get a future benefit, because investment in the means of production must precede the production, savings must be accumulated for the investment, and savings represent present consumption foregone. The point here is not that under Marxism people must give up something in order to invest for a better future, but (1) they live under the monopoly control of the Communist Party and therefore cannot share in the decision as to how *much* present consumption they will forego in favor of *what* future benefits (the Party decides) and (2) under Marxist conditions, an extremely *high* rate of savings has been forced upon the people, as Table 1 indicates.

[2] For a discussion of the failure of the Russian populace, as distinguished from a small upper crust, ever to imbibe the idea of freedom, and of Russia's history of violent swings between westernization and withdrawal into oriental backwardness, see Marc Slonim, *An Outline of Russian Literature*. Mentor Books, 1959, pp. 17-27.

payments for their services.[1] Even in the totalitarian state the slow accretion of public resentment must in time be dealt with. If police terror methods have already driven the public to the point of exhaustion, resentment can only be dealt with by increasing rewards. This last is what underlies the development of the second force: unless a timely shift is made from the stick to the carrot, the result will be a creeping paralysis of economic effort. This shows itself in operation in Soviet agriculture. Although terrorism has been halted, incentives have not been increased enough to encourage good work or to create enthusiasm. Rewards must at some point be stepped up *if the state and the Party are to go on increasing in strength and in consolidation of power*. This point was apparently reached in Russia in the late 1940s and early 1950s. Stalin kept the lid on until his death, but his successors showed that they felt an urgent need to relieve and soothe the Russian people, and to begin paying them something on account for their long martyrdom under Stalin's Marxism.

Create Communist Man

Where the buildup under socialism has been considerable, the output of goods and services becomes high enough to permit the people to begin having a bit more, that is, to begin improving their standard of living, without seriously cutting into the state's profits. In fact, the loosening up may very likely increase the state's profits: free world studies show that as the workweek went down to 48 hours, productivity went up. The Marxist state is likely to reap a similar benefit as it provides more leisure, more income and more to buy with the income.

But there is a danger to the state that has as its fundamental objective the preservation and consolidation of sole authority in a single political party. It is very much the same danger as the reigning powers in Oliver Twist's orphanage felt instantly when Oliver asked for more gruel. It was not that the resources of the orphanage would be overwhelmed if Oliver got a second cup, or even if everyone got more. The shocking thing was the challenge to the Establishment: its notion of what was enough had been gainsaid.

Under such circumstances, the question is how to yield to

---

[1] See Inkeles and Bauer, *The Soviet Citizen.*

non-constituted authority without impairing the Establishment's claim to be the font of all wisdom, and therefore, the seat of all authority. This is the problem even where, as was the case with Stalin's successors, constituted authority sees not only that the opposition force is strong, but also calculates that production would actually be increased by yielding. The problem was how to bow to the need and demand for material benefits without yielding any of the authority of the CPSU.

The Russian Marxist authorities are trying to solve this problem by the prescription that only a "new man" guided by "communist consciousness" will be eligible to live in the fully communist society. There, one will be impelled to work only by a love of work and a sense of duty, since everyone will be supplied with all he needs (rather than with what his work earns him). Such abundant per capita consumption implies an extremely high rate of per capita output, so everyone must work, and must work very effectively. As the New Program's description of the condition of true communism emphasized, "Communist production demands high standards of organization, precision and discipline..."

The New Program added:

> The (Communist) Party is the brain, the honor and the conscience of our epoch. . . .
> The period of the fullscale Communist construction is characterized by a further enhancement of the role and importance of the Communist Party as the leading and guiding force of Soviet society.
> Unlike all the preceding socio-economic formations, Communist society does not develop sporadically, but as a result of conscious and purposeful efforts of the masses led by the Marxist-Leninist party. The Communist Party, which united the foremost representatives of the working people and is closely connected with the masses, which enjoys unbounded authority among the people and understands the laws of social development, provides proper leadership in Communist construction. . . .[1]

That is, the "New Man" can be reared and imbued with his consciousness of how to conduct himself in the ideal society by the Communist Party, and only by the Communist Party. The CPSU got the following directives, in the New Program, for instructing the uninstructed.

---

[1] *New York Times*, August 1, 1961.

The Party considers that the paramount task in the ideological field in the present period is to educate all working people in a spirit of ideological integrity and devotion to communism, and cultivate in them a Communist attitude to labor and the social economy, to eliminate completely the survivals of bourgeois views and morals, to insure the all-round, harmonious development of the individual, to create a truly rich spiritual culture. . . .

The moulding of the new man is effected through his own active participation in Communist construction. . . . As Communist forms of social organization are created, devotion to Communist ideas will become stronger in life, in work and in human relations, and people will develop the ability to enjoy the benefits of communism in a rational way. . . .[1]

Resolutions adopted by the CPSU Central Committee in December, 1959, excoriated Party workers for narrowness of outlook and activity, estrangement from the masses and from production problems, and for "the taint of grayness, dryness, and of insufficient expressiveness". The new man of Marxism is not supposed to be an automaton, but, rather, a lively fellow who can get around, without danger of straying off the reservation.

We are entitled to question whether Marxism can, in a few decades, work a revolution in wayward humanity that the great ethical religions have not been able to work in millenia. We can reject the suggestion of such psycho-political alchemy as we reject the idea of metallurgical alchemy. Yet we can also recall that the serviceable arts of chemistry grew from alchemy's attempts to transmute base metal to gold. It is similarly possible that something quite serviceable in the way of political organization and economic motivation can be evolved from the communist attempt to mould a new, specifically communist, human creature:

In a sense, Marx and Engels foresaw the threat of a New Class arising, and that the threat of social differentiation was not forever exorcised by the revolutionary establishment of a classless society. Right from the *Communist Manifesto* they demanded and predicted that intellectual and physical labor cease to be the specialties of different people; and, in the same vein, the abolition of the difference between town and country. There was to be one type of communist man: dreamer and empiricist, scientist and worker, humanist, artist, huntsman, fitter,

---

[1] *New York Times,* August 1, 1961.

tinker, tailor and all — replete with Socialist Consciousness of course, and working for the joy of it alone.[1]

Unless the Marxist society *can* produce a highly serviceable type of closely controlled and amiably disposed human being, "dreamer and empiricist, scientist and worker, humanist, artist, huntsman, fitter, tinker, tailor and all" there can be no full communism ever, as presently conceived.

At the best, it is a very long term task. To the CPSU, this means that its tutorial dictatorship can stretch indefinitely into the future. This is a prospect the Marxist leaders of Russia may find more congenial than they would find the prospect of withering away, as Marxist theory obliges the Party to do once it has succeeded in moulding a nation of communist men. Lenin said that the transition to true communism could only be gradual. Perhaps we should expect the just and perfect Russian Marxist society to be always arriving, never quite just and perfect enough to force the CPSU to declare itself superfluous.

The Marxist World

The Challenge of
Marxism to Russia

Beyond the bridge, in St. Isaac's Square, a cliff rose out of the mist; fronting it, (an) enigmatic Bronze Horseman loomed, holding out his green bronze arm . . . Russia, that bronze steed is your symbol! Having reared and measured the air with his eyes, the Bronze Horseman will never set down his hoofs. He will leap over history; and great will be the tumult when he does so. In those days all the peoples of the earth will scatter in panic. Voices shall be raised in horror, curses fill the air, unheard-of curses. A yellow horde of Asiatics, stirring from their age-long retreats, will redden the fields of Europe with an ocean of blood . . . On that day the ultimate Sun shall rise and dazzle my native earth. But if you should fail to rise, O Sun, then the shores of Europe will fall under the heavy Mongolian heel . . . So rise, O Sun.[2]

---

[1] Peter Wiles, "Die Macht im Vordergrund, or The Sociology of Communism Desophisticated", *Soviet Survey,* June, 1959.

[2] *St. Petersburg,* Andrey Biely. Translated by John Cournos. Grove Press, New York, 1959, pp. 71-72.

The challenge of Marxism to Russia proceeds from the most obvious, yet most significant, postwar change in communism: Russia is no longer the unique Marxist nation.

We have seen that the response of the USSR to the challenge of the Western market economy's superiority is to seek to improve the ways and means of the Russian Marxist economic system by better planning and by tentative simulation of competitive market conditions. An abundance of goods and services, and a high quality of life, are requisites of the First Great Claim of the USSR upon its times: the claim to be building the good society most appropriate to the scientific-technological character of the 20th Century. This society, we have just seen, can *only* be formed in a hard school of experience along the road from capitalism to socialism and on to the promised land of true communism. With this basic dynamic of Marxist development in mind, we are now in position to examine the Second Great Claim of Russian Marxism: that the mature Marxist society knows how to build a socialist nations system as a mold upon which a new international order will form, a fraternal society of nations all obeying one paternal law for their mutual and common moral and material growth.

The New Program set the claim forth:

> The Socialist revolutions of Europe and Asia dealt imperialism a further powerful blow. . . . There emerged a world Socialist system, a social, economic and political community of free sovereign peoples pursuing the Socialist and Communist path, united by common interests and goals and the close bonds of international Socialist solidarity.
>
> Whereas the world capitalist system is governed by the law of uneven economic and political development that leads to conflict between countries, the world Socialist system is governed by opposite laws, which ensure rapid, steady and balanced growth of the economies of all the countries belonging to that system. . . . The economy of world capitalism develops at a slow rate, and goes through crises and upheavals. Typical of the economy of world socialism . . . are high and stable rates of growth, and the common unintermittent economic progress of all Socialist countries.
>
> A new type of international division of labor is taking shape in the process of the economic, scientific and technical cooperation of the Socialist countries, the coordination of their economic plans, the specialization and combination of production.

102

The Communists consider it their prime duty to educate the working people in a spirit of internationalism. . . .[1]

The USSR assigns itself room at the top of this more perfect international structure. This was rather awkwardly noted in the New Program:

The fact that the Socialist revolutions took place at different times and that the economic and cultural levels of the countries concerned are dissimilar, predetermines the non-simultaneous completion of Socialist construction in those countries and their non-simultaneous entry into the fullscale construction of communism. . . .

In building communism, the peoples of the Soviet Union are breaking new roads for mankind, testing their correctness by their own experience, bringing out difficulties, finding ways and means of overcoming them and selecting the best forms and methods of Communist construction.[2]

Much the same claim to the supremacy of the CPSU in world Marxism had been laid down in the Moscow Manifesto of 1960. But in reporting to the Party on that meeting, Khrushchov took care to spell out the position of the CPSU (and by virtue of the CPSU's position, Russia's place) in a way aimed at keeping leadership from becoming all obligation and little privilege. He said:

The CPSU in reality does not exercise leadership over other parties. . . . All communist parties are equal and independent. . . . The role of the Soviet Union does not lie in the fact that it leads other socialist countries, but in the fact that it was first to blaze the trail to socialism, is the most powerful country in the world socialist system, has amassed a great deal of positive experience in the struggle for the building of socialism, and was first to enter the period of comprehensive construction of communism. . . .[3]

In May, 1964, the USSR called in a statement in *Pravda* — the newspaper of the CPSU — for a "voluntary union" of "likeminded people" in a world communist system in which no single national party would exercise "hegemony". This responded to

---

[1] *New York Times,* August 1, 1961.

[2] *New York Times,* August 1, 1961.

[3] Khrushchov, "For New Victories of the World Communist Movement", report to the CPSU hierarchy, January 6, 1961. Soviet Home Service Radio, Moscow, January 19, 1961.

Russia's need to rally around itself allies Russia could depend upon in its ideological and power-politics dispute with Red China. Nevertheless, the USSR statement went on to stress ideological *unity,* not the ideological variety desired by the East European advocates of Marxist polycentrism. The need for ideological unity had become especially great, *Pravda* declared, because there were many new recruits to Marxism, "including the petite bourgeoisie of the developing countries of Asia, Africa and Latin America (which) are joining the world revolutionary forces."

And, *Pravda* went on to say:

> Without ideological unity, Communism would cease to be a world movement and become an amorphous conglomeration of parties incapable of joint action.[1]

Under this policy the leaders of non-Russian communist countries, who urge that there should be many centers of Marxist ideological authority — polycentrism — could clearly have certain national frills and characteristics in their Marxism. The bitter experience with Yugoslavia taught post-Stalin Russian Marxist leadership that a little well considered polycentrism could strengthen Russia's position while rigid centrism could weaken it. But unity was still the word. It was the word that had always been used by the CPSU to justify Russian Marxist primacy. There was no reason to think the reality of Russian Marxist centrism had been dropped by the CPSU, however more discreetly it was to be insisted upon in the face of polycentrist thought in the provinces and in the presence of Russia's need for allies against China. Khrushchov's successors told the world soon after replacing him that for them too the key idea in the conduct of world Marxism was unity.[2]

Polycentrism notwithstanding, it remained the obligation of others to recognize the fact that longer experience, military supremacy in the Marxist world, and superior economic strength are circumstances that place Russia ineluctably at the head of the

---

[1] *New York Times,* May 10, 1964.
[2] *New York Times,* October 20 and October 27, 1964.

parade in the Marxist world. Leadership goes with that position, and with leadership goes primacy. Russia is chief Marxist law-giver, ratifier, rectifier, overseer, prompter, teacher and mediator. It is Russian Marxist thought that says upon what doctrines Marxism will be unified. These are plain national advantages for Russia, and it is to Russia's further advantage to have her Marxist leadership writ carefully defined and prudently limited. But it would be crass to think only of the national advantages to Russia in being the first (however many equals there may be) in world communism: there are advantages also for international communism.

As the pioneer communist state, Russia has learned much from experience. Russia has the advantage in experience of having made and survived many grievous errors as well as the advantage of having brought off great successes. It must be assumed by Marxist managers elsewhere that the Russian managers of communism do in fact know their business. We must assume that for the most part non-Russian communist leaders (except, perhaps, the Chinese) constantly find themselves, at the bottom of disputes with the Russian leadership, concluding that Russian advice is likely to be the soundest operative Marxism. They cannot escape the fact that the most successful communist policy has a Russian context.

Nevertheless, Russia's experience gives her no immutable advantage. Time shifts situations away from the circumstances unique to Russian leadership experience. As time passes, all communist leadership comes more and more to share a common body of experience, to have views for which all can claim a practical basis. As we have noted, in recent years there has been a trend toward national communism (polycentrism) which has seen Yugoslavia, Albania and Red China declare complete ideological independence of Russia while Rumania, Poland and others[1] have

---

[1] On November 6, 1964 the *New York Times* reported from Prague:

Czechoslovakia has begun a radical overhaul of her entire economic system that is certain to produce profound though gradual political changes as well.

Under pressure of a severe economic slump and after failure of other liberal economic reforms the government has now decreed a total assault upon planning and management techniques developed in the Soviet Union and long considered synonymous with Communism itself . . .

(Footnote continued on next page)

demanded increasing command over their own economies. *Consequently, as change erodes the leadership advantage to Russia of having been the first, Russia must more and more depend for primacy in the Marxist world on continuing to be the foremost.*

Soviet development policy has therefore sought to keep Russia foremost in the Marxist world, by being well ahead of other Marxist nations in making progress toward:

1. Military parity with the United States.
2. Economic parity with the United States.
3. A standard of living equal to that of the United States.

These are the goals we saw previously in terms of the challenge of the West to Russia. Inside the communist world they are the challenge, to Russia, of Marxism.

Russia is the successful Marxist state, in terms of having survived for five decades, and in terms of having reached a higher state of military and economic strength than any other Marxist state. Russia must continue to demonstrate to other Marxist nations that Russian experience and theory make up, together, the quickest and surest communist way to security and prosperity.

(Footnote continued from preceding page)

As now envisioned, central planning will consist of little more than predicting market and production opportunities here and abroad and choosing among major trends of possible developments . . .

The essence of the new system (to become the basis of a long-term plan for 1966-70) is to replace the interest of (production) enterprises in meeting fixed production quotas with an interest in promoting their own profits (through the use of prices and wages based mainly upon the forces of supply and demand) . . .

Price policies will reward technical innovation and depreciation policies will encourage the abandonment of outmoded techniques . . .

Foreign trade will be reorganized by commodity groups. Enterprises using imported raw materials will have to take into account their real costs. Experiments will be used to determine whether certain enterprises can in effect manage their own foreign trade . . .

Enterprises will be allowed to reduce their work forces. Unprofitable enterprises will be subsidized for only limited periods.

Price ceilings and competing foreign products will be used to check efforts to raise prices faster than productivity.

Prices are to reflect production costs and, with some reservations, the relation between supply and demand . . .

The principal impetus for the adoption of the new system . . . has been the state of Czechoslovakia's economy in recent years. The volume of industrial production last year (1963) fell below the poor 1962 level. Labor productivity and national income have remained static . . .

There was no way to reverse the trend because central planning could control only quantity, not quality. It could not enforce technological improvement, innovation and refinement, which depend upon the producer's interest in his goods . . . (parenthetical matter added).

106

The most commanding demonstration would be a continuing, perhaps even widening, gap between Russia's standard of living, Russia's military capabilities and Russia's economic strength and those of the other communist nations. *This would seem to make it certain that inequality among communist states will continue indefinitely.*

The Marxist
Bloc

The community of Marxist nations is called by communist writers the Communist Commonwealth, Socialist Nations System, or socialist camp. The Marxist nations are most often referred to in the West as the Sino-Soviet Bloc, the Soviet Bloc, or just the Bloc. The main economic characteristics of the Marxist world are outlined in Tables 7 and 8.

Taken altogether, the Marxist world contains a third of humanity, and over a quarter of the world's land area. The Communist Commonwealth touches upon the land masses of South Asia and the Middle East. Only the Middle East separates it from Africa. These areas on the borders of the Marxist world contain most of the free world's population that lives in underdeveloped countries, and most of the land area of the underdeveloped free world. The rest of the underdeveloped free world, except for some of the Pacific Isles, lies in Latin America. There, one nation — Cuba — has been taken over by communism. Marxism is a force in a number of other countries of Latin America. On its West, the Marxist world borders on Europe, in fact includes the eastern tier of European nations. On its East, the world of Marxism runs on to the Sea of Japan.

About half the people of the free world live in industrialized countries, and half in underdeveloped countries. About a third of the people living under communist governments are in the USSR and the other industrialized Marxist nations, in Eastern Europe. Nearly all the rest live in communist China's tremendous poorhouse.

The Marxist Bloc is not the list of countries that Marx would have chosen. Far from it: according to Marx's analysis of capital-

107

ism, the *developed* nations of Western Europe should have led the way into communism. Marx's analysis indicated that communism should come about through a process in which capitalism develops as far as it can, breaks down due to increasingly severe contradictions among the interests of the laboring masses and the owners of land and other capital,[1] finishes its own destruction in competition-gone-mad in the form of imperialistic wars, and finally surrenders the means of production to an enraged proletariat[2] that has lost all faith in the capitalistic process.

No such thing happened. Industrialization did not anywhere breed the free choice of communism. Disappointed in their hopes and alone in a world Marx never meant for them, Russia's communist leaders had to gather their own confidence, hew out a communism for an underdeveloped, rather than a developed, nation, and seize what part they could of a world that misguidedly would neither produce communism in a developed country nor

[1] "Karl Marx contended that the value of a product is determined by the labor which goes into it, for even capital was considered to be the result of previously performed labor. Goods are, however, actually sold for more than labor is paid for producing them, and hence the difference falls into the hands of capitalists. This is the surplus-labor theory of value" (and the basis of the "contradiction" between the interests of labor and capital that Marx thought must grow ever more severe and must finally tear the capitalist world apart). Shepard B. Clough (except parenthetical addition), in *The Economic Development of Western Civilization* (McGraw-Hill, New York, 1959) p. 374.

George H. Sabine, a leading American student of Marxism spelled this out in his Telluride Lectures, 1957-58 (Sabine: *Marxism*, Copyright 1958 by Cornell University, quotations used by permission of Cornell University Press) which may be summarized as follows:

Marx established an evolutionary concept of society but became so hypnotized by the revolutionary concept of change that he disregarded his own theory of social progress. Marx thought, wrongly, that "legislation was almost powerless to regulate the economy" and that "uncontrolled exploitation would cause the poor to become continuously poorer and the rich to become continuously richer, until society was polarized between a proletariat that had nothing to lose but its chains and a parasitic capitalistic class that did no useful work ... a middle class was doomed to extinction".

On the contrary, "What industrial technology creates socially is an enormously enlarged middle class" that uses the legislative process to achieve changes and reforms that obviate revolution. The conclusion: "Communist Marxism, so far from being the social philosophy and the politics of a highly industrialized population, is on the contrary a philosophy and a political movement exerting an enormous attractive force in non-industrialized or economically backward societies, which have been mainly agricultural or peasant."

[2] The proletariat is the wage earning class, people without capital. The peasantry is not included in the proletariat since peasants live by what they sell, not by what they earn as wages. The USSR is seeking to make the peasantry of Russia into a proletariat by converting collective farms, where peasants get their income through the sale of the crops or animals they grow, to state farms, where workers are paid for their work in the form of wages.

flock to Russian Marxist leadership. After World War II Stalin plucked from the eastern borders of Europe such territory as his armies could occupy, installing communism in industrialized Czechoslovakia, East Germany and Poland, in partly industrialized Hungary and Rumania, and in backward Albania, and Bulgaria. Josip Broz Tito's independent Yugoslav communist army imposed communism in that backward country. These nations neither chose to be Marxist nor were added to the communist sphere because they were just what Russia needed. They were what Russia could get, and all she could get.

The communist parties of West Germany, Italy, France and Great Britain failed to deliver those bigger prizes: that is, Europe's principal industrialized nations, given a choice, did not choose to be Marxist.

On the east, the fantastically long stagnation of Chinese history at last ended in a communist conquest under Mao Tse-Tung. This added another backward, mainly agricultural country to the Marxist world — again the reverse of what Marx had in mind as the precondition of communism. Following the Red victory in China (1949) the Chinese Marxist leadership broke off such half-nations as it could from the northern tier of South Asia, plus one entire nation — Tibet — and added them to the "socialist camp."

It is this press-ganged crew the leaders of Marxism must try to cement into something resembling a monolith of communist faith and striving. If we are surprised at all by the amount of unrest, revolts or attempts at revolt in the world of Marxist dictatorship, it is that there has been so little overt trouble and so much apparent discipline.

East Wind,
West Wind

East Wind

I believe that present international trends have arrived at a new turning point. There are two winds in the world at present, the east wind and the west wind. The Chinese have a saying, "If the east wind does not prevail over the west wind, the west wind will prevail over the east wind." I believe that the characteristic of the trends of the present is that the east wind is prevailing over the west wind. That is to say, the power of socialism is prevailing over the power of imperialism.[1]

This homily was delivered to a November, 1957 meeting in Moscow of representatives of the communist parties of the 13 nations then making up the Marxist world. The speaker was Mao Tse-Tung, the Marxist emperor of Mainland China. The meeting resulted in a call for unity of the Marxist world against capitalistic "imperialism" and against Marxist "revisionism".[2]

The USSR was then courting Red Chinese support in the USSR's attempt to right things in the Marxist world following uprisings in 1956 in Hungary and Poland. The Hungarian-Polish outbreaks had followed hard upon Khrushchov's damnation of dead Stalin as an egocentric maniac at the 20th Congress of the CPSU (February, 1956). The denunciation of Stalin was the key move in a program aimed at improving the functioning of the USSR without loss of authority by the Communist Party. If blame for past breakdowns, failures, suffering, terror and rigidities could be focused on Stalin, the Party could be exculpated for what had

---

[1] Mao Tse-Tung, Chairman of the Political Bureau of the Chinese Communist Party (CCP) Central Committee, and as such, ruler of Mainland (Red) China, in a speech, Moscow, November 18, 1957, cited in *Chinese Communist World Outlook,* (United States Department of State, 1962).

[2] Although 13 Marxist governments were represented by their communist parties, the resolutions of the meeting are known collectively as the *Declaration of 12 Communist Parties,* since Yugoslavia, whose policies were under attack, sent a delegation to the conference but did not join in the Declaration.

The Declaration is also known as the Moscow Peace Manifesto of 1957.

The signers were representatives of the Albanian Labor Party, the Bulgarian Communist Party, the Hungarian Socialist Workers' Party, the Working People's Party of Vietnam, the Socialist Unity Party of Germany, The Communist Party of China, the Korean Labor Party, the Mongolian People's Revolutionary Party, the Polish United Workers' Party, the Rumanian Workers' Party, The Communist Party of the Soviet Union and the Communist Party of Czechoslovakia.

If the Communist Party of Yugoslavia be added, this listing provides the official style by which the world's ruling communist parties are known. In the listing, *North* Vietnam, *North* Korea and *East* Germany are meant.

The 1957 conference was officially called a Conference of Representatives of Communist and Workers' Parties from Socialist Countries. Thus, it technically was a conference of communist parties, and not of governments. This is a distinction that is often useful in the affairs of the Marxist world. It allows policy debate to go on at two levels—Party and government. Parties can be at odds, even break off with one another, while governments maintain relations, or the opposite can happen. The USSR-Red China quarrel was a dispute about Marxist policy, between the Communist Party of China and the Communist Party of the Soviet Union until 1963, when the two governments took official cognizance of the dispute. In all cases, in Marxist countries the government is the servant of the Party.

gone on previously, could appear as the originator of change to something better (not as the guilty steward doing penance for past crimes), and could ride off into a sunset future of continued CPSU power and glory.

But it took time for the idea to sink in that the denigration of Stalin was a move to strengthen the CPSU, not to weaken it. In the meanwhile there was confusion and uncertainty. In a command structure, such conditions lead to trouble. One direct result was attempted revolution in 1956 in Poland and Hungary. The outbreaks in Poland and Hungary were compounded of apparently about equal parts of belief that

(a) CPSU authority was breaking down and
(b) the nations of the West would help free them if they tried to free themselves.[1]

Mao Tse-Tung went to the clean-up, fix-up 1957 meeting in Moscow in support of the USSR which was glad to have Mao's help.

---

[1] For an account and analysis of the 1955 and 1956 revolts of Russia's East European satellites, see Robert Bass, "The Post-Stalin Era in Eastern Europe," *Problems of Communism*, Vol. XII, No. 2.

Bibliographical Note: The untiring reader of the *New York Times* will be fully informed on the long outpourings on ideological shifts, chops and shadings by the CPSU, the Yugoslav Communist Party, the Chinese Communist Party, and others, including prominently the Italian and French Communist parties that have attended defections since 1948 from complete USSR sovereignty in the Marxist world. Besides the *New York Times*, the following references can be recommended: *The Soviet Bloc,* Zbigniew K. Brzezinski, (Harvard University Press, 1960); *Marxism in Southeast Asia,* Frank N. Trager, editor, (Stanford University Press, 1959); *Readings in Russian Foreign Policy,* Robert A. Goldwin, editor (Oxford University Press, 1959); Nikita S. Khrushchov, "On Peaceful Coexistence", *Foreign Affairs,* (Council on Foreign Relations, Inc., New York) Vol. 38, No. 1, 1959; *Soviet World Outlook* and *Chinese Communist World Outlook* (United States Department of State, 1959 and 1962 respectively); *Mao Tse-Tung, Emperor of the Blue Ants,* George Paloczi-Horvath (Doubleday & Co., Garden City, New York, 1963) and many articles from 1957 onwards in the previously cited sovietological journals, *Problems of Communism, China Quarterly, Survey* and *Studies on the Soviet Union.* A major text is the New Program of the CPSU, (subsequently adopted), *New York Times* of August 1, 1961. Another major document is the Open Letter of the Chinese Communist Party, published in the Chinese Communist Party organs *Jenmin Jih Pao* and *Hung Chi* on September 6, 1963 and republished in the *New York Times,* September 14, 1963.

Problems of Communism, devoted its March-April, 1964 issue to the disruptive effects of the Sino-Soviet conflict on the Marxist world. The issue included reviews of three recent books available in English dealing with Russian/Chinese relations: Klaus Mehnert, *Peking and Moscow,* New York, G. P. Putnam & Sons, 1963; Edward Crankshaw, *The New Cold War, Moscow v. Peking,* Baltimore, Md., Penguin Books, 1963, and David Floyd, *Mao Against Khrushchev,* New York and London, Praeger, 1964.

Mao's "East wind-West wind" remark at the 1957 Moscow conference was meant as a concordant note to what, subsequent events showed, Mao hoped would be the main business of the conference: a melting down of Marxism's internal quarrels in a new, systemwide, aggressive heating up of the Cold War. His suggestion was rejected. The "Peace Manifesto" the conference produced set forth, as the key note of *world* Marxist action against capitalism, the *Russian* Marxist policy. This was the coexistence policy, championed by Khrushchov:

> The question of war or peaceful coexistence has become the fundamental problem of world politics. The forces of peace have now grown so large that there is a real possibility of averting war, as was demonstrated graphically by the failure of the imperialists' aggressive designs in Egypt. Their plans to use counterrevolutionary forces for the overthrow of the people's democratic system in Hungary likewise failed. The Communists and Workers' Parties taking part in this conference declare that the Leninist principle of peaceful coexistence of the two systems, which has been further developed in contemporary circumstances in the decisions of the 20th Party Congress, is the firm foundation of the foreign policy of the socialist countries and the reliable foundation of peace and friendship among the peoples.[1]

This expressed the Marxist Great Claim that the *existence of the socialist nations system, and only its existence, makes world peace possible.* It asserted the claim in the name of *Russian* Marxism: the coexistence policy is called a Leninist principle, and it was "further developed in contemporary circumstances" (i.e., it was given practical, contemporary, useable form) by the 20th (CPSU) Party Congress, as the "firm foundation of the foreign policy of the socialist countries".

The whole matter was debated once again in Moscow in 1960, this time by representatives of 81 Marxist parties from around the world. The result was a new Manifesto, the Moscow Manifesto of 1960, buttressed with the whole weight of world Marxism. The new declaration reaffirmed the findings on coexistence of the 1957 meeting. And the 1960 Manifesto added:

---

[1] Used by permission in *Readings In Russian Foreign Policy,* as translated in *The Current Digest of the Soviet Press,* published weekly at Columbia University by the Joint Committee on Slavic Studies; copyright—1959—by the Joint Committee. Used here by permission of *Current Digest.*

The Communist and Workers' Parties unanimously declare that the Communist Party of the Soviet Union has been, and remains, the universally recognized vanguard of the world Communist movement, being the most experienced and steeled contingent of the international Communist movement. The experience which the CPSU has gained in the struggle for the victory of the working class, in socialist construction, and in the full-scale construction of communism, is of fundamental significance for the whole of the world Communist movement.[1]

The Chinese Communes

The leaders of Marxism in China, effectively Mao Tse-Tung alone at the time of these conferences, definitively lost their bid to share world Marxist policy leadership with the USSR at these two decisive Marxist policy meetings.[2] But in place of an ideological triumph, Mao in 1957 took home to his near-starvation country of around 650 million people (at that time) something the regime needed badly and the Chinese people would appreciate more than an ideological plum: a promise of economic help from the better-off part of the Marxist world. The 1957 declaration said:

The socialist countries base their relations on the principles of complete equality, respect for territorial integrity and state independence. . . . These are important principles, but they do not exhaust the essence of relations among the socialist countries. Fraternal mutual aid is an integral part of these relations. The principle of socialist internationalism finds effective expression in this mutual aid . . . the socialist states will continue to expand and improve economic and cultural cooperation among themselves.[3]

But the relatively well-to-do Communist West failed to carry out these fraternal socialist obligations toward the impoverished Communist East. This was fateful. It brought about the division of the Marxist world into a Communist West ruled by Russia, and a disillusioned, dissenting, bellicose, needy, Communist East, ruled by Red China.

---

[1] From "The 1960 Moscow Statement" in *China Quarterly*, No. 5, March, 1961.

[2] For an evaluation of Mao's claim to be an original developer of Marxist thought, see Arthur A. Cohen in *Problems of Communism*, Vol. X, No. 6, "How Original is 'Maoism'?"

[3] "Declaration of the 12 Communist Parties", *Readings in Russian Foreign Policy* by permission of *The Current Digest of the Soviet Press*.

When it was disappointed in its expectations of aid from the Communist West, Red China challenged the Leninist mainspring of Russian Marxist policy: the "law" that a nation choosing the Marxist way of life *must* pass through a lengthy period of *gradual* improvement in the "lower" socialist stage of development, and must produce material abundance and a population imbued with communist consciousness before it can proclaim that it is entering upon the "higher" communist stage of its development.

The persistence and vigor with which the Chinese Marxists pushed this, and their "war *is* inevitable" challenge to Russia's overlordship of the Marxist world, wore down the "fraternal" relationship of the two most important Marxist nations. Dogged prosecutions of these claims finally gave Mao's "East wind-West wind" dichotomy a meaning confined to the Marxist world: that the Communist East and the Communist West must disagree, and one must prevail over the other.

The Chinese threw down their challenge to Russian Marxist primacy in 1958, when they organized China's 500 million peasants into Communes. With agriculture organized in this way, Mao and his colleagues claimed, China would make a quick breakthrough to agricultural abundance. Industry, benefitting from increased food supplies to workers and from increased and cheaper raw materials, would also raise its output and productivity rapidly, and the whole nation would be hurled ahead (ahead of Russia, as it later appeared) in a "Great Leap Forward".

Looking for the motivation of this curious and disastrous policy adventure, one specialist in Chinese affairs wrote:

> The communist leaders (of China) had previously spoken in terms of massive aid from the Soviet Union and Eastern Europe. . . . In recent years, the Soviet Union has balked at the task of giving China massive aid — hence the Communes — conceived of as a way of combining a relatively narrow capital intensive sector . . . with a large labor intensive sector which would receive little help from the modern sector, but would be bound to contribute to its growth.[1]

The Communes — Great Leap Forward experiment broke down rapidly and with great losses to China. But both ideas were

[1] A. V. Sherman, in *The Chinese Communes*.

kept alive in Chinese Marxist thought. Premier Chou En-lai called the Communes and the Great Leap ideas two of China's "three red banners" in a speech celebrating the 14th Anniversary of Red power in China, September 30, 1963.[1] Chinese publications indicated, in April, 1964, that there were some 76,000 Communes operating in 1962 and that the Commune would persist as China's primary form of Marxist farming organization.[2] However, it may continue to exist only as an organizational form, with work brigades taking over the former production tasks of the Commune.

The danger to Russia in the Commune experiment is indicated in the above quotation: the Communes and the Great Leap Forward were devices for achieving rapid economic development in a situation where capital is in short supply, agriculture is almost the only way of life, and the only abundant resource for development use is humanity. *This is Red China's situation, and it is the situation of much of Asia* (for instance, of India). *It is not the situation of Russia,* which was already industrial at the outset of Russian Marxist development. The Communes — Great Leap Forward idea, or some modification, can become the specifically Asian, specifically non-Russian route to Marxist development.

The following very brief descriptive discussion of the Communes and the Great Leap Forward can only begin to suggest the nearly unbelievable excesses and waste of resources that characterized the period in China (1958-59).[3]

---

[1] *The New York Times,* October 1, 1963.
[2] *The New York Times,* April 22, 1964. A study by Dwight H. Perkins updated Western information on Red China's agricultural output and organization, and effects upon China's industry, in *Challenge,* Institute of Economic Affairs, New York University, Vol. XII, No. 7, April, 1964.
[3] Discussion of the Chinese Communes relies mainly on A. V. Sherman, in the aforementioned "The People's Communes" in *The Chinese Communes.* Paloczi-Horvath, in *Mao Tse-Tung, Emperor of the Blue Ants* provides a graphic description of life in Mao's Communes. See D. H. Perkins, in *Challenge,* previously cited, for updating to early 1964.

The Commune idea was a response to other than the failure of Russia (and of the East European industrial communist countries) to help China. Sherman points out that the Communes, sensibly used, respond to a need to lock China's peasantry into the collectivization forced upon it in 1956-57. And Zauberman, also in *The Chinese Communes,* makes the point that, used more reasonably, the Communes might answer in part to a number of realities of Chinese life, such as the country's great labor surplus, the need to reduce the rate of population increase (segregation of men and women in barracks) and the need of China for a mechanism for mobilizing labor for

(Footnote continued on next page)

Organization of China's half a billion peasants into Communes began in April, 1958. By October, it reached a high point, at which it was officially claimed that nearly all this huge mass of people had been uprooted from an immemorial family-clan life and slammed into dormitory, mess-hall, work-gang life aimed specifically at destroying clan and family.[1]

The Commune aimed not only at collectivizing agriculture, but also at collectivizing life itself. Peasants were supposed to give up their personal plots of ground, and their food animals.[2] Every vestige of private property was to disappear. According to Chinese descriptions, the family was broken up: men and women to work gangs, children and the aged to care centers. All were supposed to eat in mess halls. In some places pots, pans and other cooking necessities were taken up to make sure all eating became collective. The day was divided into 12 hours for work, eight for sleep and four for meals. But at the height of the craze the hours for meals and for sleep were infringed upon by organized doctrinal instruction in communism. Work in some places went on until members of the work gang dropped. Everyone was ordered to do his utmost. All were promised at least a subsistence. In part,

---

(Footnote continued from preceding page)

projects, such as roads, irrigation ditching, etc., that would "capitalize" the country with the use of little capital equipment except humanity. Alexander Eckstein, writing in an issue of *American Economic Review* dealing with Red China's economy (LI, No. 2) said the Communes episode in 1958-59 gave the first glimpse of a strategy of economic development modifying Russia's strategy. This was the "strategy of technological dualism" for simultaneous development of a few highly modern, capital-intensive, large-scale industries, and of many rural, small scale, industries using little capital and much labor. The Red Chinese call it "walking on two legs". Investment funds would be concentrated mainly on developing a selection of industries capable of the largest scale output. The countryside would be forced to live mainly on its own resources, remaining in a backward condition and giving up its surplus for the development of the capital intensive large scale industries.

[1] These official claims, implying construction of mess halls and dormitories in many thousands of Chinese villages where no big buildings existed, have not been confirmed. The intent to break up family living may have been much bigger than capacity to do so. Accounts of visitors show it was done at least in some "model" communes. It may have been carried out wherever facilities for communal life existed. But this would still have left most of China's hundreds of millions of peasants living and eating in their huts, whenever they had the leisure and the food.

[2] How destructive this alone may have been was suggested by the *Statistical Handbook on Agriculture* issued in 1960 by the USSR. It said that, even after 30 years of communist collectivization of agriculture in Russia: food produced on small garden plots in Russia in 1959 amounted to 82 per cent of all Soviet eggs, nearly 70 per cent of all potatoes and nearly half of Russia's total meat and milk output, plus 45 per cent of all vegetables. (*New York Times*, Nov. 28, 1960).

labor was rewarded by money, "in part by supply according to need".

At the peak of the Communes frenzy, excited claims began to come from Party quarters all over China that the Communes were a "miraculous" success, that they were cutting through the entire building-of-socialism process, that people were rapidly (not gradually as Lenin said) acquiring "communist consciousness". As evidence there were claims that people were begging to be allowed to work without time for sleep and without regard to pay, that "miracles" of achievement were being wrought (weeks of work done in days or hours), that, in fact, China had found her way to communist consciousness and communist abundance without outside help and with almost nothing but the work of her great and patient people's hands.

Unfortunately for Mao, the Communes and, with them, the Great Leap Forward of industry, collapsed almost as quickly as they had built up.

The troubles of the communes were compounded by three successive years of bad weather, and the regime was finally forced to undertake a new reorganization of agriculture. Initially, free markets were reopened for subsidiary products. This was followed by gradual re-establishment of private plots. Finally, in 1961 the regime also began to take steps to increase individual incentives by transferring control over production and income from the communes to production brigades.

The communes continued to exist in name, but their functions were reduced to handling secondary administrative matters.

In an interview with Edgar Snow on January 23, 1964 Chou En-lai stated that the grain harvest of 1962 had been more than 10 million tons over that of 1961 and that the 1963 harvest had been higher than that of 1962 by a comparable amount, yet production had not reached 190 million tons. Therefore, the recovery was substantial, but has (1963) only reached the absolute level achieved in 1957, while, in the meantime, population has risen by 80 to 90 million people.

The harvests of 1962 and 1963, as a result, were not good enough to sustain a substantial and lopsided investment in producers' goods. Thus resources have had to be shifted, at least temporarily, from investment in capital goods industries to agriculture.[1]

---

[1] Dwight H. Perkins, "Too Much Ideology, Too Little Economics", in *Challenge*, April, 1964.

A New Asian Marxism?

China's Second Five Year Plan period ended during the time of reorganization following the Communes disaster, and the country entered upon the first year of its Third Five Year Plan. Neither the result of the Second Plan period, nor the outlines or targets of the Third Plan were announced.[1]

By 1963, however, it *had* become clear that the reorganization of Red China's economy had taken a new non-Russian-Marxist twist that could turn out to be a more sophisticated version of the Commune-Great Leap Forward idea, if China decided to make full use of it. It could, if pursued with perseverance and patience, not lately characteristic of the Red China leadership, also be a new departure in the development of Marxism, with a potential strong influence on the future of densely populated areas of Asia.

The new factor was a reversal of Russian Marxism's economic development strategy. Viewing the wreckage of the Great Leap Forward of 1958-59 the Red Chinese leadership apparently decided upon a departure in Marxist development thought *freed from the consequences of Marx's belief communism would develop first in industrial countries*. In the new Chinese strategy agriculture would come first, light industry second and heavy industry last.[2] This was called the "Walking on Two Legs Policy", a tag implying that other policies, including Russia's, go precariously on one leg only. The Communes-Great Leap Forward strategy contained the seeds of this approach, but, still at that time under the influence of Russian Marxist industrial fundamentalism, the Chinese leadership apparently thought of the

---

[1] For further assessment of the Great Leap Forward's consequences see "Some Reflections on Chinese Communist Economic Policy", *China Quarterly,* No. 11, September, 1962. Also, *China Quarterly,* No. 12.

[2] See Schran, *China Quarterly,* No. 11, especially pages 72 et seq, noting that China's *People's Daily* of April 17, 1962 made public a "Ten Assignments" policy guide for Party workers giving (1) the increase of agricultural output first place, (2) reducing emphasis upon heavy industry and increasing attention to light industry, and, (3) requiring a "contraction of the 'basic investment front' and a redirection of materials, equipment and manpower into spheres where they are needed most", plus other measures including return of people to the countryside and "further advances in planning and good work in establishing priorities for the various sectors of the economy, in the order: agriculture, light industry, heavy industry."

Communes as an indirect approach to getting a large, quick growth of heavy industry.

Late in 1963, the official *Peking Review* declared the Chinese economy to be "walking on two legs" and to be on the mend generally, although hard times were said still to be ahead. *Peking Review* credited a "gradual recovery" beginning in 1961 to the reinforcement of agriculture by manpower and capital switched from industry, to "retrenchment" of heavy industry, and to diversion of funds to water conservation and industry that is of direct benefit to agriculture. The report added that withdrawal of Soviet technicians, and "discontinuation of USSR supplies" had inflicted "incalculable losses" on China.[1]

The Bottomless Pit

It may be that from the outset the USSR leadership read "East wind-West wind" as a whispered threat. At any rate, with 1957, new commitments of USSR economic assistance to Red China ceased until 1961, when a Chinese default forced Russia to give China five years to pay off a current-trade debt of $310 million. In 1963, when all pretense of USSR-Chinese solidarity had been dropped, the Chinese disclosed that in 1957 the Russians had agreed to help China become a nuclear power. But, the Chinese said, less than two years later, when Russia's position was more secure, the USSR scrapped the agreement.[2] In the meantime, it appears that the Russians gave China nuclear help only slowly and, in Chinese eyes, inadequately.[3]

Whatever the full story of Soviet-Chinese nuclear development relations, the slowness, coldness and inadequacy of USSR economic help to Red China is clear.

The USSR is not known to have given Red China any substantial *grant* economic aid. Russia extended *credits* to Red China from 1950 through 1957 of about $1.3 billion, of which only some $790 million was economic aid. Of the total economic aid

---

[1] *The New York Times*, September 6, 1963.
[2] For the ins and outs of China-USSR-East Europe relations with respect to the USSR/China break see Harry Schwartz in the *The New York Times*, September 1, 1963.
[3] *The New York Times*, August 15, 1963.
For an evaluation of Red China's strategy of maneuver behind the USSR's nuclear shield, see *China Quarterly*, No. 2, 1960, "Communist China and Nuclear Warfare", and for China's nuclear demands on Russia, *China Quarterly*, No. 7, pp. 31-34.

$320 million was a five year loan China squeezed out of Russia in 1961 by a deficit on trade balances. China began paying these credits back in 1956. In all, from the time of the communist conquest of Mainland China in 1949, through 1962, China received only about $1¾ billion help — economic and otherwise — from the USSR, all of it in the form of credits. Footnotes 4 and 5 to Table 17 indicate that Red China has received less economic help from Soviet Russia than have East Germany, Poland or India, and that through 1962 China got only some 13 per cent of Russian aid to the Bloc and 8 per cent of total USSR economic aid credits. China has received little help from Bloc countries, other than Russia.

Throughout most of the 1950s, Red China was the USSR's single biggest trading partner. After 1959, Russia's trade with China plummeted (Table 10). China's economic development was planned around Russian material and technical help to a development core of 291 major industrial projects. The value of these projects is estimated at some $3.3 billion.[1] In addition to the sharp drop in material supplies, in 1960 the USSR further maimed China's development by suddenly withdrawing her technicians from the core development project.

In 1956-62, Red China exported to Russia over a billion dollars worth of goods in excess of what Russia sent to Red China

Bibliographical Note: These data are from Penelope H. Thunberg in *Dimensions of Soviet Economic Power*, pp. 429-430, and George S. Carnett and Morris H. Crawford, p. 474, which rounded up what was fairly reliably known about Red China—USSR economic relations through 1961. *Dimensions* brought up to date, but did not change the aspect of, earlier information from Western specialists on Red China. Some references that could be consulted on the Chinese Marxist economy in general as well as with respect to Soviet aid, are: Brzezinski, *The Soviet Bloc* (previously cited); "Supplemental Statement on Costs and Benefits to the Soviet Union of Its Bloc and Pact System" prepared by the US Central Intelligence Agency for the Joint Economic Committee of Congress for use in the Joint Committee's 1960 study *Comparisons of the United States and Soviet Economies;* Choh-Ming Li, *Economic Development of Communist China* (Univ. of California Press, Berkeley, 1959); United Nations, *Economic Bulletin for Europe*, Vol. II, 1959 and Part II, Chapter 6, 1960; *Readings in Russian Foreign Policy* (previously cited); Choh-Ming Li, "The First Decade: Economic Development" in *China Quarterly*, (previously cited), Nos. 10, 11 & 12; *The Chinese Communes, A Documentary Review and Analysis of the "Great Leap Forward"* published as a supplement to *Soviet Survey*, undated, apparently 1959, previously cited under its present title, *Survey*, consisting of analyses by Alfred Zauberman, A. V. Sherman and Geoffrey Hudson; *American Economic Review*, Vol. LI, No. 2, May, 1961; *Life in the Communes and Great Leap Forward*, SEATO pamphlets, Bangkok, 1959, and articles in several issues of *Problems of Communism*.

[1] Penelope H. Thunberg in *Dimensions of Soviet Economic Power*, p. 429.

(Table 10). This only repaid a somewhat smaller amount of USSR help in 1950-1955, but it represented a heavy outflow of Chinese resources to Russia in 1956-62, years of dire Chinese economic difficulties.

It is probably not wrong to say that Russia has done less for Red China than the Western industrialized capitalist countries did for the USSR in Russia's first stages of communist development, during the 1930s, when Russia was allowed to buy her new plant, equipment and technical training in the West.

Yet China's need is incomparably greater than Russia's ever was.

Until the Great Leap Forward catastrophe, China was making economic progress at a high rate of gain. Taking 1953 as a base, Red China had annual increases in her net domestic material product through 1957 of some 6 to 7 per cent, possibly closer to 7 than to 6 per cent.[1]

China's economic expansion in these years was two, perhaps three, times her annual population increase of about 2.2 per cent a year.[2] Consequently, there was also a high rate of per capita economic expansion. The basis for continued growth was being laid: industrial output was growing at such a pace that China's small industrial capacity may have been increasing by a fifth to a quarter yearly.

But even very rapid industrial progress is a different thing

---

[1] Choh-Ming Li, *China Quarterly*, No. 1, p. 37 et seq, for this and remainder of this topic, except as noted. A later study of "Economic Development in Mainland China", by Ta-Chung Liu of Cornell University and RAND Corporation and Kung-Chai Yeh, of RAND Corporation, in *The American Economic Review*, Vol. LI, No. 2, May, 1961 (proceedings of the annual meeting of the American Economic Association held December 28-30, 1960) found that Red China had average annual economic growth of 6 per cent a year, 1952-57 in 1952 yuan prices, and that in that period the producers' goods industry (most of industrial production in an economy that gives little attention to consumer goods) had grown at the truly phenomenal rate of 24 per cent per year. This, the authors said, had been achieved only at "terrific cost in terms of living standards" in Red China. They estimated that in 1957 per capita consumption in Red China was 11 per cent below what it was in 1933.

The previously mentioned study of the Soviet Bloc by the US Central Intelligence Agency for the Congressional compendium *Comparisons of the United States and Soviet Economies* credited Communist China with 9 per cent average annual growth of Gross National Product, 1950-1959. It said the rate of growth of Chinese industrial production, 1950-1959, was 23 per cent a year on the average.

[2] Choh-Ming Li, in *Economic Development of Communist China*, pp. 200-201, citing studies indicating this may be in the lower, not the upper, range of China's probable rates of current natural increase. China's birth rate, probably very low up to the 1940s, has been rising and her death rate falling.

from significant general economic betterment. The vastness of Mainland China's population is overwhelming. We can get a glimpse of China's bottomless pit of need as follows. Take China's gross national product in 1962 as $80 billion, her population 660 million, and assume that her economy will grow in the future at the very high 1953-57 rate of about 6.5 per cent a year netted against a population growth of about 2.2 per cent.

That is, in 1962 China had per capita income of about $121 a year, increasing, on these assumptions, at a rate (economic growth rate less population growth rate) of 4.3 per cent annually. If this highly favorable condition persisted, China would have per capita income equal to what Russia's is estimated to have been at the *outset* of Russia's first Five Year Plan ($270 in 1928) in approximately 19 years from 1962. *That is, by 1981, Red China would only be as well off in per capita terms as was Russia in 1928.* Even given the advantage of very favorable growth assumptions, China in 1981 would still be a very poor country.[1] This calculation is by no means offered as a prediction.[2] The calculation serves only to illustrate the inordinate dimensions of the economic development problem of a nation of nearly three quarters of a billion very poor people, even assuming an extraordinarily high economic growth rate operating over many years, in the presence of a high rate of population increase.[3]

---

[1] In 1960, Portugal had per capita income of $253 and Italy had $629 (US Department of Commerce, *Statistical Abstract of the United States,* 1963, page 915).

[2] An assay of "Communist China's Statistical System: 1949-1957" by Choh-Ming Li (the same as previously cited here) may be found in *American Economic Review,* Vol. LI, No. 2, May 1961. Choh-Ming Li concluded that the "best" Red Chinese statistics for the period considered were—despite efforts in China to improve its statistical reporting—only "fair", and that the best was a minority.

[3] Choh-Ming Li, *Economic Development of Communist China,* pp. 202-204: "The faster population grows, the lower will be the rate of capital formation available for raising per capita net product . . . China's rapid rates of population growth . . . pose serious problems to further economic progress. In the urban areas, the shortage of work opportunities becomes more and more pressing. Despite increased employment in factories, mines, and construction, new opportunities available each year lag further and further behind the number of new entrants into the labor force. It has been estimated that during the Second Five Year Plan (1958-1962) about five million persons will come to working age every year, consisting of 1.3 million from cities and 3.7 million from villages, whereas all the state enterprises (chiefly industrial and commercial) will be able to absorb annually about one million . . . It may be argued that more capital investment will create more jobs. But the rate of capital formation has probably been raised as far as the public can endure, as the frequent reference (in official Chinese pronouncements) to 'internal contradictions' between saving and investment demonstrates."

122

In these conditions, an "inexorable arithmetic" condemns the Soviet Union's aid to Red China to insufficiency, according to one specialist who has gone through the arithmetic.

He said:

It is arguable that the Soviet Union could not seriously commit herself to financing China's expansion without impairing her own growth. Such a commitment would certainly severely circumscribe her ability to support other economies of the bloc, let alone countries outside it, and such aid may be considered imperative for the bloc's internal strength and international policies.[1]

And yet, this analysis continued:

Taking $4,000 as the average cost of 'purchase' of employment per new entrant to modern industry (the amount arrived at by several students), and multiplying this by the potential addition to manpower of a country whose population grows by thirteen million a year, we reach an astronomical figure. Clearly, what is required for this sort of industrialization is in any case out of proportion to what can be obtained from China's domestic capital accumulation.

Russia cannot give Red China sufficient economic aid to transform her into an industrial society on the Russian model in any small number of decades. As things in China are now — a fast growing, vast population existing mainly and precariously on a low-productivity agriculture — China cannot hope to get far enough ahead of the basic needs of her population to amass capital for large *quick* industrialization. This presents China, Soviet Russia, the Marxist World, *and the world at large,* with a tremendous dilemma, of consequences that are presently unforeseeable, but obviously of titanic potential.

A student of Bloc affairs summed up:

The old monolithic unity of the Soviet Bloc is now a thing of the past. ... The most acute problem is, of course, the Sino-Soviet dispute. ... It concerns the whole orientation of Bloc policy towards the Western and

---

[1] Zauberman, *Communes,* pp. 66 and 67, citing the UN, *World Economic Survey,* 1958. See also *Soviet Economic Aid* by Joseph S. Berliner (Praeger, New York, 1958).

uncommitted worlds. The climate of Sino-Soviet relations is intimately linked to the state of East-West balance.[1]

Implications of Walking on Two Legs

China's (and perhaps the world's) dilemma is less strait, however, if the Russian approach to economic development (neglect the countryside except to squeeze it, and make "development" and "industrialization" synonymous words) is abandoned in China, and an approach more favorable to populous, agricultural countries is adopted (restrict industrialization and concentrate, at least for a preliminary period, on raising agricultural productivity). Years of frustration suffered in aping Russia's all-out-industrialization model, and in the Communes—Great Leap Forward attempt to break down the industrial development time barrier may have driven China into accepting such an approach. If Mao can be restrained from further impulsive drives to push Red China into "miracles" of Marxist development, the agriculture-first, "walking on two legs" policy could be China's salvation.[2] Pursued with a patience that the recent history of Red China could not lead one to anticipate, it could build a solid foundation for Chinese economic development of higher-productivity agricultural output. It has lately become clear that the lack of a solid agricultural base has operated to slow, perhaps limit, USSR industrial expansion. An agriculture first development policy would provide an orderly release of manpower for use in Chinese industry, would meanwhile keep people where they could be fed, would provide a growing surplus of farm goods that could be converted, through trade, to the materials and techniques of industrialization, and would provide cheap food to feed an expanding industrial proletariat in the cities.

In 1923 Lenin declared that "In the last analysis, the outcome of the struggle will be determined by the fact that Russia,

---

[1] John Keep, "Soviet Foreign Policy," in *Survey*, No. 40, January, 1962. Another thoughtful analysis of the USSR-Red China dispute in its world setting, by an experienced political writer who has lived in Moscow, may be found in Max Frankel's article on Bloc rivalry in the *New York Times* of January 21, 1963.

[2] Unless Red China is further impoverished, and its economic development maimed, by devotion of huge resources to the development of nuclear weapons. China exploded a nuclear device in October 1964.

India and China, etc., constitute the overwhelming majority of the population of the globe."[1] Lenin is an intruder in this calculation: India and China (and Indonesia, and the other heavily populated states included in Lenin's "etc.") have no need of relatively thinly populated Russia to help them make up the overwhelming majority of the population of the globe. Lenin's farsighted intrusion is rebuffed by China's new development strategy, worked out as a specific to the problems of densely populated, intensely poor, food short nations. The "Walking on Two Legs" strategy could if carried out patiently over time, not only make Chinese Marxism the Marxism of Asia. It could also exert a strong pull outside Asia. Russia appeared in 1962-63 to have difficulty keeping Castro policy for Marxism in Cuba from veering toward China. Other Latin American Marxist leaders showed signs of interest in Red China's leadership. The reason perhaps lay in perception of an aspect of the "Walking on Two Legs" policy that Chinese Premier Chou En-lai emphasized in an interview late in 1963: Chou stated that China was beginning to overcome its economic deficiencies, and emphasized that it was able to do so under its new policies "relying upon our own resources."[2] This suggested a possible escape from United States and European tutelage that is resented in Latin America, without paying what had previously seemed to be the price of such escape: inability to make economic progress.

To what extent Maoist China was prepared to rely for its future on the new development strategy could not be known outside the Chinese leadership's inner circle. All that could be known outside was the publicized fact that the "Walking on Two Legs" policy had been developed and that instructions had been issued to implement it.[3] Russia's Marxism-Leninism demands an arduous *escape* out of agriculture into industry, because Russian Marxist thought is so heavily influenced by Marx's assumption that com-

---

[1] *Soviet World Outlook*, p. 175.
[2] *New York Times*, October 14, 1963.
[3] The Walking on Two Legs Policy does not, even if it is made permanent, make China's Marxism a kind of Marxist agricultural reform movement. It is simply a way for China to use her situation and resources to industrialize in a more practical way. China appears to have the same underlying motivation for industrialization as does Russia—an urge to increase her military potential.

munism would come about first among the proletariat of the most highly industrialized countries.

As we noted earlier, Marx's error was slow to reveal its strangling effects upon the Russian economy because when communist development began Russia had a respectable industrial foundation, Russia was not densely populated and its agriculture, where some modernization had begun in the late 19th Century, was capable of producing a surplus above minimum national needs. Russia was able to use that surplus, in trade with the West, to purchase the materials and technical help for the first stages of Soviet industrial advance.

China was so much less industrialized than Russia was at the outset, her population so much more dense, and her agriculture so much less adequate that neglect of agriculture and fixation upon industry came near, in China's case, to being a fatal piece of Marxist romanticism.

A "Marxist" development strategy correcting this separation from reality would be free to develop agriculture as an instrument for industrialization. Whether or not the breach between the Russian and the Chinese Marxist parties is ever healed, the "Walking on Two Legs" revision of Marxism-Leninism could remain as a very potent consequence of the breach.

West Wind

Whatever the future of the Communist East, the contrast between conditions there and conditions in the Communist West is so great that one is tempted toward the feeling that all is well in the West. The reality is that life in Communist Europe is better than it was in the early postwar years just after the Red Army imposed Marxism, is still little, if any at all, better than it was under capitalism, and is poor by comparison with contemporary life in capitalist Europe.

An American historian, writing in 1963 on "The Post Stalin Era in Eastern Europe" said:

Manifestly, the People's Democracies (the East European satellites of the USSR) are still far from a solution of their economic problems. Comecon (the organization for economic cooperation linking them,

126

and the USSR), though increasingly active, has not yet achieved any-thing like full area-wide cooperation and specialization. No state has been persuaded to discontinue particular sectors of its own industry (in the name of the cooperative national specialization Comecon is sup-posed to bring about). Although Poland, East Germany and Czech-oslovakia have embarked upon a number of joint development projects, very little has been done so far to provide needed capital to Bulgaria and Rumania. Gross malfunction in planning of effective and equitable distribution has remained a problem in all bloc countries. Doctrinaire agricultural policies and the opposition of farmers have actually served to depress living standards, and failure to forestall fuel and power shortages has created repeated bottlenecks in industry.

Despite all these shortcomings, it is significant that the 1956 crisis (revolts of Hungary and Poland and general unrest in Marxist East Europe) did not have a long-term paralyzing effect on East European economic growth. No country, with the possible exception of East Germany, is today faced with really insurmountable difficulties. In-dustrial capacity has been increasing steadily. Living standards, while poor compared to those of Western Europe, have been maintained at tolerable and gradually rising levels. . . .

Propaganda efforts notwithstanding, each of the East European socie-ties seems to have split into two cultures: the Communist — and the apolitical, and sometimes crassly materialist, which is less and less con-cerned with aspirations that are clearly beyond attainment. The small minority seriously interested in Communism is probably dwindling, to leave the field clear for (those) whose main mutual concerns are the maintenance of personal power and the preservation of domestic tranquility.[1]

Life is better, but less meaningful, as Marxism sinks in; a gray and joyless contrast to the picture of life in Marxism's "more perfect society" dwelling in the "magnificent edifice of the new world being built by the heroic labors of the free peoples" of the socialist nations, according to New Program lyricism.

Comecon

The architects of the "magnificent edifice of the new world" of cooperative socialist nations are Soviet Russian planners. The builder is a Russian creation: Comecon (Council for Economic

---

[1] Robert Bass in *Problems of Communism,* Vol. XII, No. 2, April, 1963. Parenthical material added.

Mutual Assistance).[1] Comecon was formed in 1949 as the Marxist world's answer to Marshall Plan assistance. In later years Comecon has come to be the Marxist counterpart to the European Common Market. Comecon consists of the USSR, Mongolia, Rumania, Bulgaria, Czechoslovakia, Poland, Hungary and East Germany. Neither Red China nor her European partisan, Albania, is a member, (nor is North Korea or North Vietnam). Depending on the warmth, or chill, of USSR-Yugoslav relations (generally, the inverse of USSR-Red Chinese relations), Yugoslavia may participate in Comecon discussions as an observer, or may be absent altogether. Red China has also attended Comecon councils as an observer.

The Moscow publication *International Affairs* (not to be confused with the older British publication of the same name) gave the 20-year (to 1980) industrial and agricultural growth goals found in Table 11 for the individual Comecon countries (except Mongolia, which was let into Comecon in 1962 to keep it out of Red China's sphere of influence). Each of the planned individual industrial growth rates for 1960-1980 is below the claimed average annual industrial expansion of all Comecon countries taken together for the period 1950-1961. That is, *no Comecon country expects in the 20 years, 1960-1980, to equal the industrial expansion that the USSR says was achieved by the whole western socialist community in the 1950s. All of Western Communism is experiencing a growth slowdown similar to what we have already noted for Russia.*

Table 11 shows fairly evenly distributed industrial growth — and a common agricultural lag — in Comecon. The agricultural

---

[1] Also known as CEMA, CMEA, or EMAC, depending upon the language the initials represent.

Bibliographical Note: For Comecon, the following references may be consulted:
Brzezinski, *The Soviet Bloc;* Zauberman, *Problems of Communism,* Vol. VIII, No. 4 and Vol. IX, No. 4; United Nations, *Economic Survey of Europe,* 1959, Chapter III, and *Economic Bulletin for Europe,* Vol. 14, No. 2, 1962; US Congress, *Comparisons of United States and Soviet Economics, A Supplemental Statement* by CIA; Bass, *Problems of Communism,* Vol. XII, No. 2; Aleksandr Bilimovich, *Studies on the Soviet Union,* Vol. II, No. 2, 1962, and Roman Zybenko, the same, Vol. II, No. 4, 1963; *Bulletin of the Institute for the Study of the USSR,* Vol. X, No. 7, July, 1963; US Congress, *Dimensions of Soviet Economic Power;* Jan Wszelaki, *Communist Economic Strategy, The Role of East-Central Europe,* National Planning Association, Washington, D. C., 1959; and Frederick L. Pryor, *The Communist Foreign Trade System,* Massachusetts Institute of Technology Press, Cambridge, Mass., 1963.

lag is less evenly spread than is the common industrial progress. Only Russia and Rumania hope in 1960-1980 to see their agricultural output grow somewhat more than half as fast as their industrial production. Elsewhere in the Communist West expectations of long term agricultural progress are even more modest.

The East European communist countries have since the end of World War II followed Russia's example in planning and developing their economies. With allowances made for local peculiarities, by the early 1960s their progress was on the whole of the same order as that of the USSR and the same kind, and they were having much the same difficulties. Their worst difficulties were the same two that have become crucial to the USSR's future growth: how to develop greater economic efficiency in the planned society, and how to overcome a lag in agricultural output so serious and so general as to be a possible limiting factor on future industrial expansion.

Since 1956 Russia has been giving economic assistance to the other members of Comecon. But it was not always so.

During 1944-48 the USSR treated East Europe as defeated territory to be stripped for the benefit of the USSR. From 1948 to 1956 treatment of the East European countries was better, but still mainly exploitative. A 1959 study concluded that from 1944-1956 the USSR made away with no less than $20 to $25 billion worth of capital from East Germany, Poland, Hungary, Czechoslovakia, Rumania and Bulgaria.[1] Thus, the USSR seized from its fraternal socialist states in East Europe capital wealth of the same magnitude as the $24.6 billion worth of capital *help* the United States gave to its West European allies in the years 1945-57. The seizures were a great boost to the USSR's economic growth in the postwar era. They are a major factor in explaining why East Europe is now so much poorer than West Europe.

From 1945 through 1962 the USSR provided about $3.5 billion of economic grants and credits to its allies in Eastern Europe, about two thirds of it in 1956-62, mostly as a rescue

---

[1] By Jan Wszelaki, *Communist Economic Strategy, the Role of East-Central Europe* (National Planning Association, Washington), 1959. Penelope H. Thunberg in *Dimensions of Soviet Economic Power* said in 1962 that the Soviet removals from East Europe "in the first decade after World War II could be counted in the tens of billions of dollars," p. 427.

operation following the troubles in Poland and Hungary in 1956. The following table shows the distribution of USSR assistance to its satellites in East Europe:

USSR Economic Credits and Grants to East European Communist Countries, 1945-1962

(millions of US dollars)

COUNTRY	1945-55	1956	1957	1958	1959	1960	1961	1962	Total
Bulgaria	$198	92	72	44		162			$ 568
Czechoslovakia	48		14						62
E. Germany	363	20	260	235			475	1	1,353
Hungary	43	41	262	35					381
Poland	614	300							914
Rumania	94	95							189
TOTALS	$1,360	548	608	314		162	475		$3,467[1]

Source: Penelope H. Thunberg, in *Dimensions of Soviet Economic Power,* p. 427.
Notes: Table does not include $247 million credits to Albania.
Blanks indicate no known credits or grants.
See also footnotes 4 and 5 to Table 17.

[1]The USSR reported a credit to East Germany in February, 1962 valued at $310 million. It is believed this was part of the $475 million credit extended in 1961.

These figures include an unknown, but considerable amount of larding of what could only be called economic assistance by a stretch of the imagination. This larding is in the form of reparations, debts forgiven, and similar transactions.

The high totals for East Germany and Poland suggest the economic difficulties those two countries have experienced under communism.

Trading with Big Brother

The most obvious East European losses from political association with the USSR were in the form of war booty and reparations. But there was another large category of loss, inflicted by trading at prices dictated by the USSR. Russia charged high for Russian goods and paid low for satellite goods.[1]

[1]There has been much written in the West on this highly technical subject. It was reexamined with care by Frederic L. Pryor in *The Communist Foreign Trade System,* previously cited, (pages 144-152), where Pryor concludes:

(Footnote continued on next page)

The biggest change in USSR trade with the world since pre-war days is the fact that after World War II the Red Army delivered to Russia the mines and factories and skilled labor forces of Czechoslovakia and East Germany (as well as the lesser industrial potentials of Rumania, Hungary and Poland). The USSR can now depend upon her East European satellite sources for great quantities of capital goods. But, the longer these countries are closed off from their traditional trade lines with the West and immured in Marxist autarky, the more their technology comes to be the same as Russia's. So Russia can get from East Europe great *amounts* of capital goods, and may be able to get them cheaply, but she cannot get from her Comecon suppliers the high quality, high productivity, imports she needs to modernize the USSR industrial and agricultural economies.

The USSR forced the trade of the East European countries from its traditional orientation toward West Europe into channels that led to the USSR and the rest of the Soviet Bloc. This new and strained pattern of trade was formalized by the formation of Comecon (then known as CEMA) in 1949. The plunder of the area, rapid enforced industrialization and the strain of complete trade reorientation, created resentment and economic dislocation that led the new USSR leadership, after Stalin's death in 1953,

(Footnote continued from preceding page)

"Economists in the West have often claimed that price discrimination exists in intra-CMEA trade (especially by the USSR) . . . Although Soviet economists have proclaimed loudly that this is not the case, the price differences may be seen by examining average unit prices of some chief exports of Bloc nations . . .

"Although there are many ways to analyse the absolute price discrimination, I believe this can best be measured by comparing the terms of trade which the various East Central European nations obtain from the USSR to the terms of trade which these nations receive from each other for the same goods. From examination of economic influences in trade prices it seems quite likely that the USSR has been able to obtain an absolute price advantage from the other Bloc countries because of the trade dependency effect (the USSR has been the largest trade partner of all other Bloc nations since early post war years) and also because the USSR has been, in all probability, the largest 'single supplier' in the Bloc.

"The hypothesis that the USSR had a trading advantage over the other CMEA nations seems . . . confirmed up to 1956. It is impossible to draw a completely firm conclusion after 1956.

"Although the formal basis of intra-Bloc prices were the prices existing on the Western markets, these were difficult to determine for those goods for which transportation costs or quality differences were important or for those goods whose prices fluctuated a great deal. In these cases a price indeterminacy existed, and factors of economic power became important. Bargaining advantages were secured by political methods as well. Although Bloc trade officials played sweet tunes of proletarian internationalism in public, they practiced price discrimination in private."

to relax the most severe controls, revise the most discriminatory pricing arrangements, and lighten Russian demands somewhat. Not enough was done — if enough could have been done at that date — to avoid a series of uprisings beginning in East Germany in 1953 and culminating in national revolts in Hungary and Poland in 1956. The 1956 events led the USSR to show the carrot and hide the stick in its economic relations with East Europe.

The USSR agreed, in Comecon councils, to undertake a creative role in the economic development of East Europe. Also, debts were cancelled and discriminatory pricing was abated to the point that Russian negotiators had to be prepared to support assertions that the prices they suggested were in fact "world" prices.

After 1960, Russia appeared to be trying to develop a political and economic partnership relation with its East European allies. But the basic facts of the relationship resist a shift to partnership and tend to impose a willy-nilly exploitation of the People's Democracies by the USSR. This arises from the huge disparity in the size and economic and military strength of the USSR and its allies. Exploitation is almost ineradicable when, as in Comecon, the balance of military power is so lopsided.

Building the Magnificent Edifice

In the 1948-1956 period, much industrial capacity was built up in East Europe, but commensurate arrangements for supplies of fuels, raw materials and power resources were not made. The fact that the USSR did not divert enough of its own industrial supplies to the new East European industry to keep it from sagging was one of the contributing factors in the 1956 revolts. In 1957-58, new trade agreements were negotiated assuring East Europe of more adequate supplies for its industry, and of markets for its goods, as well as food for its growing city work force.

Comecon was reorganized, to become a planning and clearing-house organization directed toward the total integration of the East European economies with that of the USSR. Here, too, Russia has lately been trying to develop a partnership relation

132

with its East European satellite allies, but, as in trade, disparities of size and strength, both economic and military, impose a willy-nilly exploitative relationship that is next to impossible to eradicate so long as Russia feels impelled by her position in world affairs to remain world Marxist primate, and regards her military borders as being on the free world frontiers of her European allies.

Table 12 compares the economies of the East European countries, taken together, with the economies of the USSR, the European Economic Community and the United States. The table shows that in Eastern Europe the Soviet Union has an economic ally of no mean proportions. Steel production is about half as great in relation to population as in Western Europe. Electric power output approaches that of Western Europe. Grain production is half again as great with respect to population. Eastern Europe does nearly half as much trade, per capita, as does Western Europe, the world's most intensive trading area, and East Europe's trading capacity complements Russia's weakness in trade.

Each of the East European countries has a five or seven year plan for economic development. These plans were roughly synchronized with Russia's in the late 1950s. They all end, as does Russia's current Seven Year Plan, in 1965, after which more closely integrated planning is contemplated. East Europe's national economies have been achieving good growth under Marxism, and, each to itself, should continue to do so. The difficulty lies in accomplishing, under Marxism, that which Marxist policy demands fundamentally: strengthening of the socialist nations *system,* by achieving a close knit of the various national socialist economies into a system-wide whole capable of drawing the maximum benefits from large scale production for large markets.

In June, 1962, Comecon representatives conferred in Moscow and adopted a set of "Basic Principles for the International Socialist Division of Labor".

The Basic Principles were:[1]

1. Economic cooperation in Comecon based upon international division of labor.

---

[1] Based upon *New York Times,* June 17, 1962. Oskar Lange had earlier proposed principles for economic cooperation in Comecon very similar to the rules Comecon adopted in 1962.

2. Promotion of division of labor through long range planning.
3. Comecon countries should specialize and subcontract among themselves, mainly in machinery making, production of chemicals and in metal production.
4. Organization of division of labor with an eye to a high degree of economic efficiency and of labor productivity.
5. Specialization should be planned to fit in with the all-round development of each national economy.
6. Comecon should have as an overall aim the reduction of differences in the levels of development of the member countries.
7. In practice, economic cooperation should be achieved through long term trade agreements, bilateral and multilateral.

Khrushchov took up the Basic Principles as a step toward achieving for Marxism, through Comecon, those economies of scale that he had observed operating under capitalism:

> If we now, throughout the whole socialist system, unify our planning by organizing mass production, the profitableness of which is already proved by capitalism, we shall in this way undoubtedly hasten our victory in economic competition with capitalism.[1]

But Marxism is held back from completing its proposed "magnificent edifice" of international socialist cooperation and common economic growth by the same Marxist-imposed difficulties in achieving economic efficiency we have already seen operating in Russia. Autarkic national economic aims, price systems set to meet the fiscal requirements of planning goals rather than being derived from economic realities, the lack of a freely operating interest rate to indicate where investment is needed, all tend to block the flow of economic signals. This blinds planners to what is or is not efficient, what is or is not needed, and condemns the system to find its way by blind reckoning along a path of economic experimentation that is expensive, uninformative and slow.

The Basic Principles call for economizing on the use of labor and material resources by joint investment. This and the other cooperative arrangements under the Basic Principles were aimed at putting an end to national autarky. Comecon seeks to substitute for national autarky a system-wide autarky that would make the Communist West in effect one economy. It would be as nearly

---

[1] Kommunist (Moscow) No. 12, 1962, Page 16, cited by *Studies on the Soviet Union* Vol. II, No. 4, 1963.

sufficient to itself as possible. It would produce within the system where it is most efficient to produce (except for the USSR, which, pleading its defense responsibility, reserves the right to have facilities for every type of production within the protection of its own frontiers).

But, every Comecon country has its own price system, established to respond to its planned national growth objectives, not derived from its particular supply and demand situation. Every Comecon country has similarly arbitrary wages and taxes. These are not coordinated with the prices, wages and taxes of neighboring Marxist countries. These arbitrarily derived prices, wages and fiscal policies do not, in fact, efficiently and objectively serve the cause of economic growth, either national or Comecon-wide. Consequently, decisions as to where it would be most efficient to locate new jointly financed production facilities become a matter of intuition or, at the best, informed guesswork. Each country fears to lose out in this gambling game, and joint investment has consequently proceeded only very cautiously.

Similarly, the Comecon Basic Principles state that the practical instrument of Comecon economic integration should be increased trade.

The trouble with this is that each country is in effect a closed unit, locked in with its own economic plan. The national plan earmarks each product in advance of production for a specific use within the plan. Trade takes place only as an adjunct to the plan (if something from the outside is needed, the plan must provide for the production of a surplus of salable goods of equal value that can be traded for what is needed), or as a diversion from, and probably a frustration of, the national plan.

True organic trade would work differently. It exerts an influence on economic processes at work within the economies of trading partners. Trade among fully planned economies does not permit this benefits-of-trade process to work. Consequently, the use of trade as an instrument of integration in Comecon would appear to be frustrated unless and until common, systemwide planning can take place. But effective allocation of the use of resources on a systemwide basis through one common plan would run into the same difficulty as joint investment: it would require prices with realistic meaning, wages corresponding to differences in productivity; in fact, *integration of Comecon would seem to demand the same simulation of the capitalist market — or market socialism — that the USSR seems to need and to be groping toward.*

It is perhaps due to these practical difficulties that socialist fraternalism does not seem to yield, necessarily, any higher inclination toward international economic cooperation than occurs elsewhere. Rumania (and to a lesser extent, Hungary and Poland) has broken with the Comecon scheme of Russian dominated integration in the Communist West. Under Comecon plans Rumania was to be an essentially agricultural country that also had a large petroleum industry. Rumania edged somewhat toward the Red Chinese in 1962-63. Rumania became the first nation of the Communist West to reestablish diplomatic and economic relations with Albania, suspended by the USSR and others in Comecon in December, 1961, after Albania attacked the Khrushchov regime on China's behalf. In the first half of 1963 Rumania concluded new commercial arrangements with Peking, apparently feeling that China's vast needs offered a market that Russia and the rest of Comecon could not (or, due to rigidities imposed by the unresolved Comecon conflict between national and system-wide planning, would not) duplicate.

Rumania simultaneously increased business dealings with the West, ordering parts from France for a steel mill Russia was to have supplied but did not, and contracting for iron ore in Brazil and increasing her trade with Western Europe generally.[1] Rumania's declaration of economic independence was capped in mid-1964 when Rumania negotiated large scale trade arrangements with the United States.[2]

The Weakest Spot Everywhere: Agriculture

The agricultural brake on Comecon's progress can best be described by saying that the situation in the East European countries is apparently no better than in the USSR. Like Russia, the East European Marxist states have, so to speak, been "walking

---

[1] See "Rumania Steps Out of Line," in *Survey*, No. 49, October, 1963.
[2] See *New York Times* June 2, June 3, June 9, July 15, and July 23, 1964.

on one leg" and find themselves precariously situated in consequence. Their cities are filled with a new proletariat tempted in from the countryside without much regard to the manpower needs of agriculture, to provide labor for high flown national plans for quick industrialization. The food and raw materials supply for this growing urban population is not increasing fast enough.

Wladyslaw Gomulka, Marxist leader of Poland, probably spoke for all of communized and collectivized East Europe when he told the Central Committee of the Polish Workers' Party at a meeting in February, 1963:

> Agriculture is the weakest sector in our national economy. Last year, as we know, we had a bad harvest: this failure had an immediate and considerable effect upon the foundations of our entire economic plan for 1963. . . . There is no doubt that we must strengthen our weakest member.[1]

In 1962, Czechoslovakia reported that she fell 12 per cent short in fulfilling her agricultural output plans, while her industrial expansion plans were 99 per cent met. Premier Antonin Novotny told the Twelfth Congress of the Czechoslovak Communist Party:

> Gross agricultural production has on the average between the years 1958 and 1962 failed to rise and is hovering around the position it occupied before the war.[2]

Bulgaria, (which attempted, but failed, in 1962 to advance her agriculture by a "Leap Forward" of 25 per cent), Hungary, Rumania and East Germany also had records of poor agricultural progress.

Bulgaria, Hungary, Czechoslovakia and Poland responded mid-way through their development plan periods ending in 1965 by jacking up the percentages of their national income to be invested in agriculture.

Rumania and East Germany were the exceptions. East

---

[1] *Bulletin* of The Institute for the Study of the USSR, Vol. X, No. 7, July 1963, "Comecon Agriculture in 1962," Stefan C. Stolte, for which also most other data in this summary of Comecon's agricultural situation.
[2] *Bulletin* of The Institute for Study of the USSR, as before.

Germany was apparently depending upon continued heavy Russian assistance. Rumania scheduled a 17 per cent increase in agricultural output, but a 6 per cent *decrease* in investment in the means of farm production. Despite agriculture's obvious need Comecon's overall plan, like Russia's, continues to stress investment in industry.

We began this examination of communist man and his communist world with the lyric promises of the New Program of the CPSU as to what a communist world would be like. We took a look at the indeterminate *via dolorosa* of "socialism" on which, and only on which, according to Leninist Marxism, the "higher" society of communism can be learned and earned, and along which the indispensable "new man" equipped with "communist consciousness" is to be produced under the tutorial dictatorship of the Communist Party. We looked at the challenge that communism presents to Russia to justify and maintain its overlordship of the Marxist World by being first to enter the "higher condition" of communism.

We found that the Marxist world is divided into its own East and West. Two factors are common in the Communist West: agricultural stagnation and slowdown of industrial growth. Agricultural stagnation may be placing a built-in limit upon Soviet economic expansion toward the abundant society required for true communism. In the rest of the Communist West also, agricultural failure under Marxism has slowed, and is also seriously limiting, further economic progress. Russia's East European satellites are edging toward political independence of Russia. Poland and Rumania have achieved considerable economic freedom.

The Communist East is dominated by the tremendous mass of Red China — nearly three quarters of a billion people, increasing at something like 14 million souls a year, sunk in poverty so deep that China's relatively prosperous socialist ally Russia has drawn back in dismay from serious economic entanglement.

138

Nevertheless, it is possible that China's astronomic need, Russia's refusal to help, and China's disastrous failure to crush the means of fast industrialization out of her peasants may have guided Chinese development policy toward a new and more promising Marxist strategy. China's "Walking on Two Legs" strategy could have special appeal (a) to her populous fellow nations in Asia, which, like China, have little to grow with except the labor of their unskilled farm people, and (b) to all underdeveloped nations, in Asia and elsewhere, that would place special value upon a development strategy freeing them in a measure from dependence upon the technological support of the developed countries (as China claims to have freed herself from Russia).

It may be that two conclusions are justified:

1. The slowly but surely gathering long term consequences of long time addiction to the industrialize-and-let-agriculture-be-damned theory of economic development may indefinitely hold the USSR and the rest of the Communist West back from that triumphant passage from socialist hardship to communist abundance (or something like it) that the CPSU's New Program tells us will attract the world to Russian Marxist leadership.
2. But ironically, the degree of industrialization and scientific and cultural advancement that Russia *has* achieved, together with her rigid prescription of development by way of continued concentration on industry, may be moving Russia, in the view of the world's poorer masses, toward the position of a luxury purveyor of economic development.

At any rate, there would seem to be no place in the Marxist world with any prospect soon of producing Peter Wiles' "communist man: dreamer and empiricist, scientist and worker, humanist, artist, huntsman, fitter, tinker and all . . ." because the Communist East is too constrained by agricultural poverty and the Communist West is too addicted to agricultural neglect.

III. The Strategy of Competitive Coexistence

When the Soviet people will enjoy the blessings of communism, new hundreds of millions of people on earth will say: "We are for communism". It is not through war with other countries, but by the example of a more perfect organization of society, by rapid progress in developing the productive forces, the creation of all conditions for the happiness and well-being of man, that the ideas of communism win the minds and hearts of the masses.[1]

One Way
World

Marxism claims to be a later, higher and better organization of human activity than is capitalism (which, in the Marxist view, overthrew and replaced feudalism because *it* was, in its time, a later, higher and better form). *Ipso facto,* Marxism claims, it has a right, *and a duty,* to succeed capitalism wherever it can, by the most convenient means, and as soon as possible. By the same Marxist lights, it can justifiably impose itself by the dictatorship of the proletariat and without the consent of the governed, because Marxism regards itself as being good for the governed, even if the governed have not yet come to see it so. And finally, all the foregoing being given in Marxist reasoning, it is clear to Marxists that once a country is taken over, Marxism has the same right and duty to prevent the return of that country to a lower form of organization that it had to seize it in the first place.

Thus, the one way world.

We will not be diverging from our subject matter if we pause briefly to examine this concept, political though it is, because the one way world view is the kingpin obstacle to genuine and lasting

---

[1] The New Program, *New York Times,* August 1, 1961

settlement of any issue, great or small, including economic issues, between the United States and the USSR, and between capitalism and Marxism.

So long as Russian Marxist policy is based on the view that wherever Marxists manage by whatever means to gain control, a "law governed" historical process has taken place that must be regarded as sacred to the well being of mankind, and, as such, must never, by any means, be reversed, *there is no such thing as peaceful coexistence, there is only hostile coexistence.* War begins where diplomacy is blocked: the Cold War between the USSR and the free world exists because the one way world view is a view that cannot be worked into the checks and balances by which diplomacy maintains international equilibrium.

It was this hostile, rather than peaceful, view of coexistence that permitted Khrushchov and his colleagues to try to slip assault rockets into Cuba in October, 1962, while still maintaining that the essence of Russian foreign policy was peaceful coexistence. Here, too, the reasoning was based upon the superior good, in Marxist eyes, of Marxism. The New Program stated that:

> Soviet experience has shown that socialism and peace are inseparable. . . . The Soviet state, which champions peace and implements the Leninist principle of peaceful coexistence, is a mighty barrier to imperialist aggression. . . .

> Communism accomplishes the historic mission of delivering all men from . . . the horrors of war, and proclaims peace . . . for all peoples of the earth. . . .

> A grim struggle is going on between two ideologies — Communist and bourgeois — in the world today. This struggle is a reflection, in the spiritual life of mankind, of the historic transition from capitalism to socialism.

> The CPSU considers that the chief aim of its foreign policy activity is to provide peaceful conditions for the building of a Communist society in the USSR and developing the world socialist system and . . . to deliver mankind from a world war of extermination.

> Imperialism is the only source of war danger.

> The consolidation of the Soviet state and the formation of the world Socialist system were historic steps toward the realization of mankind's age-old dream of banishing wars from the life of society.

142

To abolish war and establish everlasting peace on earth is a historical mission of communism.[1]

This states the Third Great Claim: that Marxism (and only Marxism, as practiced by Soviet Russia) can reorganize international relations so that the danger of war is permanently eliminated from mankind's worries.

Our special interest is in the handmaiden of Russia's "peaceful" coexistence policy: the "competitive" coexistence policy.

It is here that the Marxist economic theory and practice we have been examining up to now, first at home in the USSR, then transferred to the Marxist nations system, turns outward and makes direct contact with us, and our world. We will look at it through the medium in which the contact is made: trade. We will look at USSR trade first as it is used with respect to the developed, industrial nations of the capitalist world, where it is an instrument to "gain time" in Russian Marxism's race to overtake capitalist economic progress, and to maintain the USSR as chairman of the Marxist world. Next, we will look at trade as it is used by Russia in an effort to enlarge Marxist influence in the world, through economic contacts with the underdeveloped nations of the free world.

Trade is Aid:

*USSR Trade with
the United States*

> It is readily seen that the policy of peaceful coexistence receives a firm foundation only with increase in extensive and absolutely unrestricted international trade. It can be said without fear of exaggeration that there is no good basis for improvement of relations between our countries other than development of international trade.[2]

The statement that "there is no good basis" for the improvement of relations between the USSR and the United States except "development of international trade" is not only uncommonly

---

[1] *New York Times,* August 1, 1961.

[2] N. S. Khrushchov "On Peaceful Coexistence," *Foreign Affairs* as carried with permission of *Foreign Affairs* in *New York Times,* September 3, 1959. Written by Khrushchov explicitly for American publication in advance of his visit to this country shortly after publication.

unqualified in Soviet international parlance. It is also an exception in another way. It is one coexistence policy point that has not been used tactically — put forward, withdrawn, amended, re-advanced, rewithdrawn, offered anew in partial form, as, for instance the Berlin issue and disarmament. This suggests that the Soviet leader may indeed attach very special importance to opening up trade with the United States.

We cannot try to decide, here, whether this is a fact. The question can only be tried by the United States government in the light of all the information and analysis available to it. Any decision to open up trade could in all likelihood be arrived at only gradually, according to Soviet responses to gradually changed trade conditions.

We can, however, explore the subject as one of at least potential, perhaps even probable, first rank importance, with a view to preparing ourselves to answer the policy question:

> What are the *terms* upon which the United States might re-open trade with the USSR, should that appear to be advisable?

Preparation for that question lies in exploration of the realities of trade relations between the United States and the USSR, against the background of what we have learned about the Soviet economy, and the problems of the communist nations system, in Parts I and II. We will try to make such an exploration here.

The Statistical Section gives particular attention to trade, in order to provide a facts and figures underpinning comparable in depth and breadth to the importance of the subject. Table 10 shows Soviet-Chinese trade. Table 12 compares total Soviet trade to the amount of trade done by the Comecon nations, the Western European nations, and the United States. Table 13 shows what are the main items of USSR trade, and how the emphasis of Russian trade shifts according to whether the trade is with one or another of the components of the communist world, or is with the free world industrial countries, or the free world underdeveloped countries. Table 14 narrows the focus to the critical item of USSR trade in machinery and equipment. Table 15 shows the relative importance, in terms of dollar amounts, of USSR trade with the parts of the communist world, with the developed and underdeveloped countries of the free world, and provides USSR, United States and world total trade figures as yardsticks. This table also shows Russia's trade balances with all the main trading areas of the world. Table 16 gives a country by country view of the trend of USSR trade since the Soviet economic offensive began in 1954. Table 18 shows USSR (and other communist world) trade balances with the underdeveloped free world countries. Table 19 shows year by year changes in free world trade with the USSR, and other communist areas, since 1947.

Why
Russia Wants
to Trade

A United States Congressional study of 1962 assessed the motives of USSR trade with developed capitalist countries:

> Soviet economic intercourse with industrialized non-Communist countries has always represented a time-saving device, for trade has made possible a rapid shift away from a primitive to a modern, more productive technology in a large number of industries. So long as some part of the Soviet economy lags technologically behind the West, the USSR will always have available a ready device for buoying its growth rate through imports. In shifting to a more advanced — i.e., more productive — technology, the Soviet Union borrows all the resources, including time, that must go into the research and development of more efficient techniques.[1]

That is, Russia wants to trade with the developed capitalist countries in order to acquire quickly and cheaply the machinery, equipment and human know-how that embody the world's highest technology.

The Technical Need for Technology

> . . . under the leadership of the Party, the Soviet people have reached such summits . . . that our country now has the opportunity of entering a new, important period of its development, *the period of extensive building of communist society.*

---

[1] *Dimensions of Soviet Economic Power,* p. 430.

145

The principle tasks of this period are to establish the material and technical base of communism, to further strengthen the economic and defensive might of the USSR and, at the same time, to provide for the fuller satisfaction of the growing material and spiritual requirements of the people.[1]

This was the assignment that Khrushchov gave to the Russian people in laying before them the Seven Year Plan for Soviet development in the period 1959-1965. He continued:

The fundamental problem of the coming seven years is to *make the most of the time factor* in socialism's peaceful economic competition with capitalism.[2]

How was Russia to make up ground on the United States, running so far ahead of the leading Marxist society? By modernizing quickly, through the use of high productivity technology:

The present level of socialist production does not as yet enable us to create the abundance of material and cultural values necessary to satisfy the rising requirements of our people and ensure their harmonious development. But communism is impossible without that. Consequently, the first job is further to develop the production forces and step up the production of material values. Communism is feasible only if we surpass the output levels of the leading capitalist countries and raise labor productivity far above that of capitalism . . .

The most important thing is to make the best use of available material resources. It should be brought home to every single worker that we can overtake and surpass the leading capitalist countries in per capita output only if we surpass their productivity levels in industry and agriculture . . .

At present, productivity of labor in US industry is approximately two to two and a half times higher than ours, and about three times higher in agriculture.[3]

If Russia's living standard goals, her need for military parity with the United States and her deficiencies in economic efficiency are considered in company with one another, it is clear that trade for the best of the world's production technology is not for Russia a matter of convenience, it is a necessity. This means large scale importation of machinery and technical know-how.

---

[1] *Control Figures,* p. 19.
[2] *Control Figures,* p. 21, emphasis added.
[3] *Control Figures,* pp. 117-118, and 141-142.

146

There is a further need. Marxism can only lay claim to having produced a "higher" form of human society than capitalism's when it can provide more and better goods and services for its people. But superior consumption (per capita) cannot come forth from inferior production (per capita). So *the key to Russia's advance out of capitalistic-like socialism to the "new society" of communism free of all "remnants of capitalism", is sharply rising productivity, both industrial and agricultural.* Russian productivity is so much below the productivity of American labor because American labor is better educated and has more and better capital equipment, in industry and on the farm. Russia can only gain ground *rapidly* on the United States by the quick acquisition, and extensive and intensive use, of technology at least as high as that of the United States, put to use by management and a work force at least as adept as ours. Without *quick* gain from imported technology, an "inexorable arithmetic" condemns to failure Russia's exertions to lift the most advanced Marxist state above the United States, because the United States economy is also growing. United States economic growth is massive, even though its growth rate is not exceptionally high, since the base for growth (the size of the United States economy) is so big. This arithmetic is suggested in Tables 2 and 4.

Russia can, and does, obtain much of the technology known to the capitalist world in trade with Western Europe and Japan. Nevertheless, the Soviet leadership has, clearly, been convinced that the USSR urgently needs full access to *United States* technology. Since they have trade access to most non-American technology they presumably have what they consider pressing reasons for nevertheless wanting to trade with the United States also. Russians, like others, can and do read our technical publications and patent descriptions, and copy. But copying is slow and expensive, only a long step less so than full scale development from scratch.

And, it is not only time that is at stake. We have seen that Russia is giving serious consideration to the introduction of price and profit signals into the operation of her Marxist economy. Trade could be helpful in two ways. First, the Russian leaders, locked up in a closed planning system, cannot tell what investment decisions (including how and where to use new technology) and which, if any, of their centrally determined prices are the right ones. Trade could be used to give the planned, nerveless, Soviet economy a sense of being in touch with competitively determined investment and price policies. This could be accomplished by permitting some amounts of Western goods to enter Russia, and be sold there in competition with Soviet goods, on a continuing basis. This would open the Soviet planning chamber's windows to Western competitive pressures, perhaps permitting, at no ideological cost, better economic decisions and improved economic efficiency in Russia. Second, it is a particular gain for Marxism, in a race to overtake capitalism, to be able, through trade, to avoid not only *Marxism's* propensity to err in the use of new technology, but to avoid also the losses incurred by capitalism in discovering *its* errors. This gain is achieved when technology is imported that is already fully understood and evaluated.

It is by no means certain that Marxism can work out a market socialism (or some other simulation of the competitive capitalist market) that can be stomached by the Communist Party and will still permit a reasonably close approach to the investment efficiency of a high class capitalist economy. If simulation of the market turns out to be impossible for the USSR, large scale, continuing import of Western machinery embodying the technological fruits of the West's competitive economic processes, could turn out to be the alternative to large-scale defection from Marxist ideology.

Khrushchov did not feel it indelicate to affirm the USSR's need to a group of Western businessmen, at a trade fair in Leipzig in March, 1959. The Russian leader said that strategic restraint of trade with the USSR

> ... has cost us a great deal, because we were forced to introduce in a great number of branches of industries the manufacture of new products which, if there were no restrictions on trade, we could obtain from other countries where these products have been manufactured efficiently for a long time, and which one could buy at a mutually advantageous price.[1]

---

[1] Berlin Radio, March 9, 1959.

It will be useful to take note of the following four points at this juncture:

1. A great deal of the flow of technology from one to another part of the *capitalist* world results not so much from trade alone as from investments flowing across international boundaries. The counterpart to this, in the case of the USSR, is the hiring of foreign technicians to install new equipment and train Russians in its use.

2. Our friendly trade partners, in Western Europe and elsewhere, do have "normal" trade access to the US, yet their productivity lags behind ours, in general. Although there are other than technological reasons for their lag, it nevertheless suggests that the process of closing a technological gap is extremely difficult, even under the best of circumstances.

3. We do not deny rapid economic growth to the USSR when we deny her trade access to US technology. Witness the USSR growth rate since World War II. But, as any nation modernizes economically, its gains become more and more dependent upon extensive and skillful use of advanced technology. Also, there is, as indicated by Table 4, a vast difference between rapid economic growth, and catching up with a country whose productivity is far ahead. *It is catching up with the US, not rapid economic growth, that is next to impossible for the USSR in the absence of large scale imports of advanced US production equipment and know-how.*

4. Access to the US equipment market could not of itself cure Russia's economic weakness. Only improved USSR economic management can do that. But access to advanced US technology would make the cure more of a possibility.

Technology and Russia's Political Needs

We noted in Part I that Russian failure to shoot past capitalism's best economic attainments in the near future could go little noticed and perhaps unmourned among the Soviet people. The reason was that the Russian people might nevertheless be receiving very important improvements in their living standards.

But Russia's Marxist leaders cannot be satisfied with such a modest victory. First, contentment among the Russian people is not the aim; the aim is to provide a better standard of living to the Russian people as an incentive to them to keep hard at work toward the political goals their leaders have selected.[1] Also, so long as Marxism is intent upon world supremacy and so long as Russian Marxism is intent upon dominating world Marxism, Russian Marxism must try to excel the United States. Russian Marxism must likewise face constant ideological challenge from within the Marxist world.

Thus, for political ends of (1) enlarging the influence and size of the Marxist world, and (2) dealing with ideological claims from within the Marxist world, Russia's over-ambitious aim of catching up with and excelling United States economic performance is a practical tool in the hand of the CPSU leadership. This is nonetheless true even though it may not be possible to overtake the United States within any foreseeable time.

United States Restraints
on Trade with
Communist Countries

During 1948-49 the Marxist world, then under Stalin and Mao Tse-tung, destroyed the basis for cooperation between the capitalist and the Marxist worlds established during World War II, and embarked upon the Cold War. The free world learned of this through the elimination of non-communist influence from the governments of the East European countries and the establishment of communist dictatorship in Mainland China.

Among the results of this betrayal of free world cooperation with the communist countries in World War II was the establishment by the United States of trade controls designed to protect United States resources and to deny strategic goods to the communist countries.

The distinction between goods of military value and of no

---

[1] In the more primitive conditions of Red China, "Good Feelingism" is a danger (of relaxation) actively combatted by the Party. Russia has arrived at the point where some good feeling is thought by the Party leaders to be necessary to further hard effort. The setting of goals so high as to be unattainable is one way of keeping satisfaction with improving conditions from melting into a relaxed euphoria, because, so long as the goals are not reached, there is an excuse for withholding an extraordinary part of the nation's income for further capital investment. This also has the political benefit, for the Party, of justifying indefinitely continued Party supervision of the national effort.

150

or little military value is difficult, because capacity to produce military and consumer goods is at bottom the same. This is especially the case with the USSR and other communist countries, where there are shortages of most things. In such a situation, an increase in capacity to produce steel, for example, is needed for both refrigerators and guns. The making of war, together with the prosecution of the Cold War by such means as building dams in Egypt, steel mills in India and rocket emplacements in Cuba, has become such an all embracing business that it is difficult to think of an improvement to a nation's productive abilities that would not have strategic implications.

The United States has consequently taken a broad view of the "strategic" trade to be denied to the Marxist countries. A Senate study published in 1961 described United States restrictions.[1]

In brief:

All trade (exports and imports), and financial transactions with Cuba,[2] Red China and her Asian satellites is forbidden.

The export to communist countries, in general, of strategic goods or goods in short supply is forbidden, and other exports are under special, discriminatory treatment.

There are five principal laws:

1. The Johnson Act of 1934, with amendments of later years, forbids other than the usual commercial short term credits to nations in default on debts in the United States, unless they belong to the International Bank for Reconstruction and Development (World Bank) or the International Monetary Fund (both United Nations institutions). How long is "usual" and "commercial" in credit terms depends on the goods involved: from 180 days (for light goods) to five years (for heavy, long-lead goods). Bloc nations are not members of either of these organizations. The USSR is in default of Czarist debts, debts for relief work in Russia after

---

[1] *United States and World Trade, Challenges and Opportunities,* Final Report to the Committee on Interstate and Foreign Commerce, US Senate, by the Special Staff on the Study of U. S. Foreign Commerce, March, 1961, p. 92.

[2] Cuba is permitted to receive some U.S. food and medical supplies, but may not export anything to the U.S.

World War I, and for Lend Lease supplies during World War II.[1]

2. The Trade Agreements Extension Act of 1951 stripped most-favored-nation treatment from communist countries, except Yugoslavia. Other communist countries must pay full 1930 tariff duties on their exports to this country (that is, they do not benefit from the generally applicable provision of United States trade laws that exports of any country are treated the same as we treat the same exports of the country with which we have the most favorable trade arrangements).

3. United States control of exports to communist countries developed out of the Export Control Act of 1949. Under this law the Department of Commerce exercises a general supervision of all exports, to any country, through an export licensing system. The Export Control Act established two principal reasons for denial of exports:

   a) To avoid depletion of short supplies.
   b) To regulate the sale to communist countries of materials regarded as having strategic significance.

Under the Export Control Act any export, except to Canada, must be licensed. The granting of a license is automatic except for the export of materials in short supply or of strategic significance. These are specified in a "Positive List" kept up to date by the Department of Commerce. Exporters may ship goods on the Positive List to any but communist countries after doing no more than *applying* for a license. That is, even for goods on the Positive List, the granting of an export license is automatic except when the destination is one of the communist countries.

In the case of communist countries except Yugoslavia, Poland and Rumania, these Positive List goods can only be shipped if a license has in fact been granted. Poland has had more liberal treatment since 1957 and Rumania was given access to most United States goods in 1964. In both cases, the exceptions were meant to encourage the satellite country to continue upon a course of increasing economic independence from the USSR.

4. The 1917 Trading With The Enemy Act was applied to halt all trade with Red China, North Korea and North Vietnam.

5. The Mutual Defense Assistance Control Act of 1951 (the

---

[1] *United States and World Trade*, p. 93.

Battle Act) attempts to enforce the United States controls upon free world countries by calling upon the President to deny continued United States assistance to any country permitting export of strategic goods to the communist countries if the denial would be in the best interests of the United States. This is so hard to interpret, and so hard to apply in ways that are not more damaging to the United States than to others that the penalties of the Act have not been used.[1]

Most other nations, including all other major industrial countries, have rejected the complete United States embargo on trade of any kind with the Communist East, confining restraints, if any, to a list of strategic goods less restrictive than that of the United States. By 1964 our industrialized allies were moving rapidly toward trade with the USSR, Red China and East Europe under minimum restraints.

The USSR's Shopping List

As soon as the USSR leadership under Khrushchov had the main lines of the Seven Year Plan (1959-65) laid out, Khrushchov sent a Soviet shopping list to President Eisenhower.[2] Since then neither the passage of time nor changes in Russian leadership have diminished Russia's need for high technology imports. If anything, the slowdown in the Soviet economy, and agricultural stagnation, have re-emphasized Russia's need to get help from trade with the United States.[3] Nor has the mix of goods Russia wants changed: the emphasis is still on acquiring petro-chemicals production equipment and know-how, and upon similar goods

[1] For details see Releases of the Department of Commerce, Bureau of International Commerce, of September 2 and 3, 1964, titled "East-West Trade," "Yugoslavia-U.S. Policy," "Export Licensing Policy Toward Poland and Rumania" and "Export Licensing Policy Toward Cuba."

[2] See *U.S. - U.S.S.R. Trade Relations,* US Senate, Foreign Relations Committee, June, 1959, for the quotations from Premier Khrushchov's letter, President Eisenhower's reply, and related matter used in this section.

[3] Aleksei N. Kosygin, then First Deputy Premier of the Soviet Union, urged in March, 1964, upon Clarence D. Martin, Jr., United States Undersecretary of Commerce, the conclusion of a long term trade agreement with the USSR. Kosygin evaded talk of continued Russian wheat purchases in the U. S. in favor of discussion of prospects for broad trade expansion. *New York Times,* March 6, 1964.

calculated to yield the highest gains to the overall efficiency of the USSR economy.

Khrushchov wrote:

Dear Mr. President: I am addressing this letter to you, in order to take up once again the question ... of the ways and means to improve and develop the relations between the Soviet Union and the United States ... there are great and unused opportunities to solve this problem ... There is no need to dwell on the usefulness of developing economic, and, above all, trade relations between countries ... We remember, for instance, the words of the late Secretary of State of the United States, Cordell Hull, to the effect that "commerce and association may be the antidote for war." You, I believe, will agree that now, in particular ... the world is in need of such an antidote.

During the past ten years trade between the Soviet Union and the United States ... decreased to a negligible level for reasons beyond the control of the U.S.S.R. The United States is now the only great power that has no trade agreement with the Soviet Union. Individual trade transactions concluded between American firms and Soviet organizations for foreign trade are very insignificant ...

I should like, Mr. President, to emphasize particularly that the Soviet Government, in advancing its proposal for the expansion of Soviet-American trade, by no means has in mind armaments or plant equipment for military production.

The Soviet Union is now engaged in carrying out a new and extensive program for a further increase in the production of consumer goods ... directed toward further improving the prosperity of the population. The Soviet Union has all the possibilities and its own resources for carrying out this program successfully. However, in order to expedite this program, the Government of the Soviet Union could make large scale purchases of appropriate equipment and materials in the United States ...

In the opinion of the Soviet Government, cooperation between our countries in the field of production of synthetic materials and finished articles thereof could be developed along the following lines:

Purchases by the Soviet Union of industrial equipment in the United States: including complete equipment for plants and factories, conclusion of agreements with firms for obtaining licenses in individual cases, for inviting American specialists to work in Soviet enterprises as consultants on the production of certain synthetic materials, and for acquainting Soviet specialists with the production of these materials

154

and finished articles thereof. The Soviet Union, for its part, is prepared to make it possible for American specialists to learn about the achievements of the USSR in this field.

Organizations of meetings of American and Soviet scientists and specialists for discussing problems of production of synthetic materials . . . Mutual participation of Soviet scientists in the work of scientific research institutions of the United States of America, and of American scientists in the work of scientific research institutions of the USSR (concerning) new types of synthetic materials and technological processes.

At the same time the Soviet Union could propose a broad program for placing orders in the United States for other types of equipment and for the production of consumer goods, and for housing and public construction . . . refrigeration equipment; installations for air conditioning; equipment for the cellulose, paper, and wood processing industries, the textile, leather-footwear, and food industries; television equipment; equipment for the manufacture of packing materials; packing, packaging and automatic vending machines; pumps and compressors; machinery for the mining industry, for the manufacture of building materials and the mechanization of construction; hoisting, transporting, and other equipment.

In addition . . . big orders could be placed for a number of industrial materials and finished products, including orders for equipment for rolling ferrous metals, pipes for city gas lines, various chemical products, medical equipment, medicines and certain consumer goods.

The Soviet leader's letter said Russia could pay for its purchases in the United States by the sale of manganese, chromium ores, ferrous alloys, platinum, palladium, asbestos, potassium salts, lumber, cellulose paper products, unspecified chemical products, furs and "a number of types of modern machinery and equipment".

However, Khrushchov noted, the long break in US-USSR trade would make it difficult to get two way trade going again quickly; the USSR, (with its Seven Year Plan going into operation in six months) was in a hurry; so Russia would be willing to start off buying more than it sold. Consequently, Khrushchov said:

The question arises concerning possible payments in installments and making available long term credits on normal terms and conditions.

The Russian leader had one further proposal:

It is also obvious that the development of trade between the USSR and the United States will require the creation of the requisite contractual and legal basis.

This last was a demand for revocation of the United States laws forbidding most-favored-nation treatment for the USSR and her communist allies (who, Khrushchov said, would also be willing to step up their trade with the United States if US-USSR trade negotiations were successful).

The Russian shopping list was so broad as to amount to a statement of the basis, in USSR opinion, for negotiations for trade freed of *any* limitations, except on items of finished military equipment or production equipment specifically for military uses.

Khrushchov's letter dwelt most intensely upon the industry the Seven Year Plan counts upon most to give the USSR its biggest economic stimulus — the chemicals (largely petro-chemicals) industry. The petro-chemicals field of production is a United States technological specialty. It is looked upon in the Seven Year Plan (which runs through 1965) as a tree full of productivity plums, as the following excerpt from the official *Handbook* suggests:

> The polymer materials industry is to develop (during the Seven Year Plan period) on a new raw materials basis—the utilization of natural and casing-head gases. This will yield a tremendous saving, as the following example indicates.
>
> The utilization of casing-head gases instead of alcohol in the production of synthetic rubber will save nearly 1,300 million rubles in capital investment. Plastics can in many cases successfully replace lead, copper, nickel and bronze.
>
> The expansion of the production of synthetic materials will enable us to produce an abundance of fabrics within a brief period of time. The expenditure of labor on the production of one ton of cotton amounts to 238 man-days; on one ton of wool, 624 man-days; on one ton of viscose staple fiber . . . only 60 man-days.
>
> An exceptionally big savings in resources and time is made by the use of plastics in engineering . . . Thanks to their smaller specific weight, one ton of polymers can yield nearly six times as many goods as a ton of steel.

Surveying the USSR economy in 1962, a study for the United States Congress said:

... The U.S.S.R. today must import not only certain industrial materials of strategic significance, but, most important, it continues to be dependent on Western technological advance in many key industrial branches ... Despite a costly and longstanding program for the development and production of synthetics, the U.S.S.R. still is dependent on imports of natural rubber for industry and transport. A primary goal of the present plan period, the expansion of the chemical industry, is patently dependent for its success on imports of Western chemical equipment which, embodying most recent technology, serve as prototypes to be copied, adapted and perhaps even improved at some future date.[1]

President Eisenhower replied gently to the 1958 USSR trade and credit proposal:

... the United States favors expansion of peaceful trade with the Soviet Union. Expanded trade between our countries could, under certain conditions, be of mutual benefit and serve to improve our relations in general.

A period of several years of particularly strained US-USSR relations followed, arising from the then current Soviet belief that development of large rockets had given it a military edge over the United States. After the USSR learned in Cuba in the Fall of 1962 that Russia could not challenge the United States on a nuclear basis, and after the Red Chinese had made their challenge to Russian Marxist leadership unequivocal, there was some clearing of the atmosphere. This was signified by successful negotiations by the United States and the USSR in 1963 of a ban on above-ground testing of nuclear weapons.

In these circumstances, the prospects for exploration of trade as a way to "improve our relations in general" became brighter. But at that point, Marxist Russia's economic nemesis rose up ironically. Two bad harvests had been sufficient to imperil the Soviet grain stocks. No quick remedy (other than liberation of the collectivized Russian peasant) was at hand domestically to insure a permanent recovery the next year, or in any specific number of years.

Russia was forced to go into the free world's grain markets, including the United States', to make very large purchases of

---

[1] Penelope H. Thunberg in *Dimensions of Soviet Economic Power,* Joint Economic Committee, p. 413.

wheat. She paid for the grain out of her reserves of convertible currencies, and of gold. These same reserves originally were her chief hope of purchasing the technology she needs to get from the United States. Russia's agricultural deficiencies are due, as we saw in Part I, to a long history of neglect and abuse of Soviet agriculture in favor of Soviet industry. To the extent that agricultural breakdown such as that of 1962-63 continues in future years to be a threat—so long, that is, as Soviet agriculture remains basically weak—Russia will continue to be forced to hoard her reserves of currencies and gold to correct food shortages, limiting her ability to overcome her technological deficiencies by the purchase of equipment and advice in the United States. Among the technological deficiencies her agricultural weakness would thus make it harder to correct would be the deficiency of chemical fertilizer production, without which the agricultural frailty can scarcely be overcome.

Trade,
Not Raid

The counts against opening United States trade to the Soviet Union can be piled up high. The Marxist leadership declares itself openly and officially to be out to "bury" the capitalist world. To do so, it is necessary for the USSR to gain access to United States technology, without which she cannot quickly build the high-productivity system that alone could permit Russia to equal United States economic proficiency in the near future. The Soviet production system is still concentrated mainly upon serving and strengthening Russia's military-industrial complex, rather than upon improving the Russian standard of living. Marxism's long neglect and abuse of agriculture in Russia, in favor of the military-industrial sector, is showing stubborn, long-term, widespread effects tending — unless technology bought abroad comes to the rescue — to force Russia to pause, economically, to repair her agriculture. The pause could turn out to be long and costly, restraining for years the growth of the industrial base of Soviet military might, diminishing the image of youthful vigor the USSR seeks to create, thereby eroding Soviet prestige in the world.

158

Each of these can be taken as a reason for not giving the USSR greatly increased access to United States technology, materials and technical advice. Together, they form a strong negative.

There is an even stronger, and purely practical, negative: as things stand, Russia has little to sell us that the United States needs or wants to buy from the USSR.

Yet, in the shopping list Premier Khrushchov sent to President Eisenhower the Soviet leader suggested trade turnover (exports plus imports) "amounting to several billion dollars . . . over the next several years". If this is taken to mean, say, $3 billion (to give "several" its smallest possible number) over a period of five years (giving "several" a large number) the proposal would seem to be for something not less than $600 million a year of US/USSR trade.

This would make US/USSR trade about twice the size of the largest Soviet trade turnover with any western country in 1962, when USSR trade with the West was higher than ever before. It would be more than seven times as big as US/USSR trade turnover in the peak year up to 1962 (see Tables 15 and 16). Trade of the size apparently proposed would make Russia a major trading partner of the United States: US/Soviet trade would be about a tenth as big as trade turnover with our largest trading partner, Canada, about a fifth the size of annual trade with our next most important partner, Japan, about half the size of annual United States trade exchanges with Italy or France, and approximately the same as United States trade turnover in 1962 with Colombia, Switzerland, or the Philippines.[1]

If Russia is to step up her trade with the United States to

---

[1] See Table 1211, *Statistical Abstract of the United States, 1963,* US Department of Commerce (1964); see also Table 15 and 16, Statistical Section of this study, showing total USSR trade with all free world industrial countries in 1962 of $2.4 billion (a record) and that USSR trade turnover with any single industrial free world country, except Finland, was less than $350 million in 1962 ($44 million in the case of the United States). See also Table 1, *Trade Negotiations for a Better Free World Economy,* a Statement on National Policy by the Research and Policy Committee of the Committee for Economic Development, New York, 1964, showing the smallness of the share of the communist countries as a whole in world trade ($17 billion exports by communist countries out of world exports of $123 billion in 1962 although the communist countries have a third of humanity) and the high concentration of communist trade on intra-Bloc exchanges ($11.5 billion intra-Bloc exports out of total Bloc exports of $17 billion in 1962).

anything resembling the level the Soviet leadership apparently believes to be necessary to "gain time" in competition with the United States, Russia must find a way to pay for the purchase of large amounts of high technology equipment, and the materials and advice that go with them. This could be done in the following ways:

1. Russia could finance the expansion of trade with the US by long term dollar credits large enough to cover her proposed purchases. Russia would then have the problem of meeting the repayment schedule.

2. Russia could pay her dollar debts out of the proceeds of Soviet sales in other hard currency countries. That is, Russia could use any net balances she acquired of French francs, German marks, British pounds, etc. to buy dollars, and use the dollars so acquired to square her accounts in the US. This would be "triangular" financing of the dollar credits. Russia could dip into her reserves of gold to help make annual repayments of such long term dollar credits.

3. Russia could finance expanded trade with the US in the same way most trade is usually financed, by earning dollars through the sale in the United States of goods and services.

Credit

Khrushchov proposed in his shopping list letter to President Eisenhower that Russia's purchases in the United States be financed by "long term credits" on the grounds that at least initially Russia would be buying more than she sold to the United States.[1]

The proposal suggested that the Soviet leadership had in mind an assistance package deal with the United States: Russia would come in with a list of wants, in the form of proposed purchases of United States equipment, materials and technical advice extending over some fixed number of years, say, five years; the United States would be asked to extend to Russia credits covering most, or all, of the total cost of the proposed purchasing program, repayable over a larger number of years, say, 12 to 20 years (which latter is about the limit for credit on

[1] Discussion of long term credits for the USSR must proceed on the assumption that Russia had satisfied the provision of US law, mentioned earlier, forbidding extension of more than normal commercial credits to nations in default of debts in the US.

equipment purchases). The package would be an overall agreement only, put into practice in the form of many purchase and credit agreements with many suppliers and creditors, of various sizes and kinds, but adding up to the total outlays proposed and conforming to an agreed annual debt repayment schedule. Russia would have to satisfy United States creditors that she would — and could — pay her debts.

If it is supposed that Russia could buy the equipment, materials and advice the Soviet leaders feel they need to get from the United States for about $3 billion, and if they were able to arrange to finance these purchases over a 12 year credit program, the annual cost (including 4 per cent interest) would be some $315 million. If (which may be more likely) Russia's needs from the United States would come instead to not less than $5 billion, annual repayments, over 12 years, would be close to $526 million. If repayment for $5 billion purchases could be spread over 20 years, at 5 per cent, the annual cost would be around $396 million.

It therefore appears that Russia would need to be able to foot annual payments somewhere between $315 million to over half a billion dollars if she were permitted to finance a large scale modernization program in the United States through long term credits. Russia's ability to pay such debt installments would presumably increase with any increase in the productivity of the Soviet economy resulting from importation of high technology production equipment and methods. Her ability to meet her obligations in a credit program would depend upon what dollar amounts she could make available out of the other possibilities we mentioned for financing her purchases in the United States: the use of dollars acquired by the conversion of Soviet earnings in other hard currencies, the use of gold or currency reserves, and earnings from sales of Soviet goods and services to the United States.

Triangular Payments

To whatever extent Russia could amass currencies that are convertible to dollars (i.e., "hard" currencies) she could use the dollars so acquired to pay for current purchases in the United

States, or to pay off United States credits. This would be "triangular" financing of USSR trade with the United States.

The following table suggests how much Russia, and her East European satellites, might be able to make available for such purposes. It shows USSR and other Comecon trade with the COCOM countries. COCOM is a 15 nation body called the Coordination Committee of the Consultative Group, which is the free world organization charged with coordinating imposition of restraints upon trade with the Sino-Soviet Bloc. The COCOM nations are the chief source of currencies convertible to dollars in large amounts on a regular basis. It is therefore chiefly in trade with the COCOM countries that the Communist West would have to scrape together any foreign exchange to be converted to dollars for the purpose of expanding trade with the United States.

The table indicates that the USSR could not look to the hard currency earnings of the Communist West for large scale help in financing USSR trade expansion with the United States. The East European satellites ran trade *deficits* with the West in most years from 1957-1962. The average net dollar equivalent of the foreign exchange earned by the Communist West in dealings with COCOM countries, 1958-1962, was only $101 million. In the three years 1960-1962, the annual average was just over $68 million. Since the above figures include trade with the United States, they are what would be left over for triangular financing of any *expansion* of USSR trade with the United States.

It is at best a slim reed upon which to rest a large scale, long term program for trade expansion. And, in actuality, even these small balances might not be available. This is so because their availability would depend upon the willingness of European countries to permit the communist countries to sell to Europe, year after year, more than they bought from Europe, and *then let them use the European currencies thus earned to purchase American — not European — goods and services*. Whether an extensive trade program, especially, a long term credit program, could be built upon expectations of such magnanimity seems very doubtful.

162

**Hard Currency Balances Arising
From the Trade of the USSR and
the Other Comecon Countries with
COCOM nations.***

(millions of dollars)

	USSR	EAST EUROPEAN SATELLITES[2]	EUROPEAN BLOC
COCOM COUNTRIES:			
1958 Exports to	$451.9	$ 916.0	$1,367.9
Imports from	539.8	926.4	1,466.2
*COCOM Balance[1]	—87.9	—10.4	—98.3
1959 Exports to	435.1	1,067.8	1,504.9
Imports from	696.7	1,010.1	1,706.8
*COCOM Balance[1]	—261.6	+59.7	—201.9
1960 Exports to	722.9	1,251.5	1,974.4
Imports from	838.1	1,211.6	2,049.7
*COCOM Balance[1]	—115.2	+39.9	—75.3
1961 Exports to	821.4	1,354.5	2,175.9
Imports from	952.4	1,289.4	2,241.8
*COCOM Balance[1]	—131.0	+65.1	—65.9
1962 Exports to	897.5	1,398.2	2,295.7
Imports from	1,015.2	1,344.2	2,359.4
*COCOM Balance[1]	—117.7	+54.0	—63.7

SOURCE: Department of State, *The Battle Act In New Times* (1962) and The Battle
Act Report of 1963 (1963), Tables 3A & 3B.
*COCOM=U. S., Canada, Japan, Belgium, Denmark, France, West Germany, Greece,
Italy, Luxembourg, Netherlands, Norway, Portugal, Turkey and United
Kingdom.
[1] *Minus signs* indicate foreign exchange available to the Bloc (arising from COCOM
purchases exceeding COCOM sales).
Plus signs indicate Bloc foreign exchange balances owing to COCOM countries (arising from COCOM sales exceeding COCOM purchases).
[2] East Germany, Poland, Czechoslovakia, Rumania, Bulgaria and Hungary.

The USSR's Gold Reserves

How much Russia has in the way of monetary reserves —
gold, dollars and currencies convertible to dollars — is not known
with any certainty. How much gold the USSR mines yearly, or
could mine, is also unclear. In recent years, Russia has sold
abroad an average of about $250 million of gold annually. Some
Western authorities have taken this to be a rough index of how
much gold the USSR is mining yearly. The United States Bureau
of Mines estimated USSR gold production at $350 million in

163

1958, and said that production had been between $300 and $350 million a year since 1950.[1]

In the spring of 1964 the USSR announced that gold mining (chiefly placer mining, in Siberia) had been started two weeks earlier than usual, and that new, more productive equipment was being put into use. This announcement was apparently intended to assure Western authorities that the USSR would have gold available to pay for her 1963 and any future grain purchases in the West. Russia is known to have sold some half a billion dollars worth of gold through the end of 1963, and her sales continued at this twice-normal rate through the early months of 1964.

Russia is probably the world's second biggest gold producer (after South Africa). Most of Soviet production is in subarctic far east Russia, where transportation and other production costs are high and work can go only seasonally. Russian gold production costs, therefore, may be high.

> (USSR) gold holdings were last reported as $840 million in 1935. In the period 1936-59, these holdings were increased by gold obtained from Spain during the Civil War, amounting to more than $500 million, and by production, estimated at from somewhat less than $5 billion to somewhat more than $7 billion; and they were reduced by sales amounting to at least $2 billion. The combination of these estimates would suggest that Soviet gold holdings at the end of 1959 were in the range of $4.0 - $6.5 billion.[2]

Since 1959, the outflow of gold from the USSR has not diminished. Beginning in 1963, agricultural failure forced Russia at least to double drawings from her gold reserves and gold production. Even if Soviet gold output has been forced up to an average of around $400 million a year (an increase of a third over the highest average production, 1936-59, suggested above and by the United States Bureau of Mines for the 1950s) it seems unlikely, in view of the drains upon the Soviet gold stock in recent years, that at the end of 1963 Russia would have had a gold reserve of

---

[1] US Department of the Interior, Bureau of Mines, *Minerals Yearbook,* issues of 1947 through 1958. These and other, lower and higher, estimates of Soviet production were cited by O. L. Altman in International Monetary Fund, *Staff Papers,* April, 1960 issue, "Russian Gold and the Ruble," which is the primary source of the data presented here on Soviet gold output and reserves. The article rounded up what is known in the West.
[2] O. L. Altman, "Russian Gold and the Ruble," in *Staff Papers,* International Monetary Fund, April, 1960.

larger than some $7 billion.[1]

Russia must continue to finance trade deficits (for herself and for others in Comecon upon occasion) with gold. She also needs large amounts of gold for conversion to many currencies to pay for the upkeep of her embassies around the world, and to finance the high costs of espionage. Russia must use gold for all these purposes, over and above any favorable trade balances, because the ruble is not convertible to other currencies in world markets. USSR trade-aid commitments in many underdeveloped free world countries have been greatly expanded. The cost of espionage rises in a time when defense rests upon a scientific revolution. The costs of staffing and operating embassies also rises in a world in which the number of countries, and the number of things about which embassies must learn, increases steadily. All these factors suggest that Russia's year-to-year needs for gold will rise, not decline. To the extent that Marxism's failure to achieve a high productivity in agriculture persists, Russia (and her creditors) must always have it in mind that one or two bad crop years would send the USSR back into Western markets, gold in hand, to purchase food for the Soviet Union and its allies.

Paying for Trade With Trade

The foregoing leads in the direction of rejecting Russian suggestions that she be permitted to finance a large expansion of trade with the United States through long term credits, because Russia's ability to generate either the foreign exchange, or the gold, with which to make annual payments running to several hundreds of millions of dollars a year over the next decade or so seems dubious.

There is a further reason that would seem also to suggest that Russia's credit proposal be turned down. This is, that refusing it would put pressure upon Russia to abandon her autarkic, one-way-world, competitive hostility, in favor of a gradual resumption of more normal relations with the United States and the rest of the free world.

How, then, *could* US/USSR trade be expanded by anything

---

[1] Estimated by taking the stock as $6.5 billion at the outset of 1960, average production of $400 million a year, four years, 1960-63, outflow $250 million 1960-62 and half a billion 1963.

like the magnitudes the Russian leaders apparently desire? There would seem to be only one practical way to finance it: by dint of trade.

This forces us back on the fact that as things stand the USSR has little to sell to the United States. For the most part, Russian production for export, (ores, furs, lumber, wood-paper products) competes with products the United States obtains from its best and biggest trade partner, Canada.[1] In 1948 Russia abruptly closed her markets to the United States for some products, such as chromium, which she now offers again. But new free world sources have meanwhile been developed for them, not only in Canada, but also in Turkey and in Africa, where the United States has large economic development commitments. There would seem to be every reason against turning away from these suppliers and handing the trade back to Russia.

Russia could earn more hard currency by stepping up sales of petroleum in the West, and Russia did increase her petroleum sales in Western Europe rapidly in the late 1950s and early 1960s. But USSR petroleum sales are at the expense of markets developed by United States (and other Western) oil companies together with Middle East and Latin American oil suppliers that we have an interest in supporting. It would seem contrary to free world interests to permit a position to be created in which the expansion of Soviet trade was chiefly financed by large scale expansion of Soviet petroleum sales in the West.[2]

Further, the potential of USSR oil exports is large but not unlimited: Russia is depending upon a switch from solid fuels to oil fuels as a major factor in future overall Russian gains in productivity. The Russians are also depending upon widespread substitution of plastics and other petro-chemical products for further hoped-for gains in the productivity of the Soviet economy. These plans require a great expansion in *Soviet* petroleum consumption, placing some limit upon Russia's ability to increase

[1] See *The Growth of Soviet Economic Power and Its Consequences for Canada and the United States.* (1959). Canadian-American Association, Washington, D. C.

[2] If only normal economic considerations applied, and Russian petroleum sales could be regarded exclusively as new competition in international markets, it could be applauded as can other sound increases in international trade competition. But as with other USSR trade, Russian petroleum exports have a political context that imposes special considerations.

petroleum production for export at competitive prices. Here again, the prudent creditor would be given pause.

This does not mean that trade between the United States and Soviet Russia cannot be expanded by increasing the exports of *both* countries. *The Soviet Union could increase its exports to the United States, if the United States government decided Soviet access to United States technology was desirable, by the same method any other country uses: by the development of products wanted in the United States, offered at competitive prices.*

This would require the USSR (and her allies) to *trade* with the West, not just grab prototypes. It would mean the development of a long run basis for continuing, steady, competitive trade, such as exists between the United States and France, West Germany, Great Britain, Italy, Japan, and so forth through the list of our free world trade partners.

This could only be successful if Russia's planners let the autonomous element of competitive market forces enter in some degree into the planning chamber. They would be obliged to find out what they could make that might sell in the United States. They would have to make it, as our trade partners do, on faith that they could sell it to us. In such a venture, there would be failures as well as successes. Soviet planning would have to become sensitive to the ever changing desires of a competitive market, and to its ever changing competitive conditions, as are the United States and all others engaged in competitive world trade.

But as we have already noted more than once, the one great untouchable in the Marxist society is the authority of the Communist Party. Permitting autonomous market forces to enter into the calculus, even in only a subsidiary degree, would be a serious invasion of the CPSU *sanctum sanctorum*. But, as we have also noted, permitting some scope in Russia for international economic competition might turn out to be the lowest-cost way, in terms of ideological erosion, to get increased efficiency in the Marxist planned society.

Trade on a continuing basis with the West, not raiding of its markets, would involve some relaxation of the autarky maintained by Marxist countries as one of their principal defenses.

167

Russia and her allies would be required to move out of the refuge of high-cost, non-competitive self sufficiency part way, at least, into the more open country of competitive economic existence.

This would be a long, and, from the ideological point of view, a frightening step to take. It could not be expected that Russia would undertake it in any one decisive, or open, move. There would be no need for Russia to do so. What is wanted is the acclimatization of Marxism to world trade, with the formation of some, at least, of the inner links and interdependencies which that implies. Russia could do so in gradual steps, each taken without any overt decision, or announcement. Each such step would nevertheless be perceptible to United States policy makers.

United States policy toward the opening of trade access to Russia and her allies of the Communist West could, under a come-out-and-trade approach, be similarly gradual and accretive. Such a policy would allow us to start small, and widen the opening only as Russian intent to engage in genuine, organic trade became clearer. The Soviet proposal for a package assistance deal, financed by long term credits, would, on the contrary, commit the United States to too much, too soon, with too little knowledge of Russian intentions, and it would deprive us of any lever with which to pry Soviet Russia out of its hostile, one way world into the competitive, mutually reliant commerce of the free and peaceable world.

What Russia learned of United States military strength and determination in the Cuba confrontation, the new dangers to Russian Marxist leadership arising from Red China, the unfolding effects in Russia and elsewhere in the Communist West of long-term agricultural stagnation, the growth in Russia of a more realistic — and therefore less optimistic — appraisal of Russia's economic position vis-a-vis the United States, all these are factors that would seem to push Russia powerfully toward getting trade with the United States open, even at a high price.

There could be no assurance that there would be no repetition of the 1948-49 betrayal of Western help to Russia in World War II, if we again extended a friendly hand. Large scale trade with the United States would strengthen Russia. With the added

168

strength would come new temptation to try to gain a world advantage for Russian Marxism by some new coup. Russia tried it as late as 1962 in Cuba. These risks would be considerably abated if any increase of US/USSR trade were based, as suggested above, on a gradual growth of mutually beneficial, self-financing commerce.

But United States calculations would also have to take into account the fact that there could be benefits to us of a high order. Russia has adopted a maverick, hostile, one way view of the world: on the grounds that Marxism is doing history's "law governed" work, Russian Marxism holds the view that all change should be in the favor of the USSR, and that any such change, once made, should be irreversible. This is the indigestible fact about Soviet Russia in world affairs. It is why Russia cannot be dealt with as other nations: the USSR harbors an intolerance that cannot be absorbed into the checks and balances of the international diplomacy the world depends upon for regulating the relations of sovereign nations. Where the effects of diplomacy are blocked, war begins. Thus, so long as the USSR insists upon a one way world, the Cold War must continue.

Nothing is less a one way proposition than genuine international trade: trade voluntarily carried on, over time. The basis upon which such trade rests is inherently two way. All the parties to trade are presumed to benefit, else, they would get out of it.

If the USSR were willing to enter into genuine, long term trade, on the basis that is common to the free world — each nation selling abroad according to its comparative advantages in production — Russia would be taking a long step away from its warhawk, autarkic world of hostile coexistence and toward the peaceful interdependence that is the free world's normal life.

Genuine international trade in effect casts the bread of all participants upon the waters of international commerce. In effect it gives hostages to the fortunes of trade. It rests upon tacit agreements that each participant will deliberately let itself become somewhat dependent upon all the other participants. No one way flow is tolerable. Genuine trade is a coordinate, interconnected process, capable of and expectant of indefinite continuation and elaboration. A rough balance in kind is kept, so that in the main

169

real goods, and human services, are exchanged for real goods and human services. Gold is used only to settle accounts at the margin of affairs.

Soviet traders, on the contrary, sally forth to buy up prototypes of production goods, and to fill temporary chinks in their planned economy, all in the interests of eventual autarky as the underpinning of hostile independence. Their trade agreements in the non-Marxist world stand aloof from the world's trade, taking the form of bilateral barter arrangements, government-to-government. Gold, rather than a commitment to continued trade, is the guarantor. Russia does not permit her centrally directed economy, or those of her allies, to schedule production dependent upon outside sources of supply, if there is any alternative. The usual alternative is the foregoing of production and consumption: Russians just do not have many automobiles, refrigerators, washing machines, and the like. Nor is it permitted to build up industry that would depend upon sales in the non-Marxist world.

It is clear that asking Russia to commit herself to genuine, long term trade, rather than to continue the raiding of world markets that has been her trade pattern, may be to ask a great deal internally as well as externally. But the Soviet Union and its East European allies critically need the technology available from the United States to build the "most perfect society" of full communism as the Marxist mold and model of man's future social organization. Building this "higher" society, we have seen, is not only Marxist Russia's supreme aim, it is also her supreme necessity, if *Russian* Marxism is to keep its place in the van of world Marxism and is to be an attraction to the nations of the world as yet undecided what system they prefer. These are needs for trade of the highest order.

It would therefore seem that the United States can accordingly demand a price of a high order: that the USSR come out and enter into the world's real trade, and that it do so consciously and deliberately, however quietly, as a step toward renunciation of the one way world. If this were to happen, a possible beginning would have been made, however discreetly, upon the establishment of conditions without which the Cold War can probably not be liquidated.

170

Trade is Aid:

*USSR Trade with
the Underdeveloped Countries*

In the early years after World War II the Soviet government followed tactics it had used since the 1920s to encourage Marxists in Asia, Africa and Latin America to bring about communist revolutions. The USSR, and the local Marxist leaderships in underdeveloped areas, were helped by the fact that European hegemony still spread over much of Asia and Africa in the form of colonial government. Most of Latin America was politically free, but felt itself economically colonized by the United States and the industrial powers of Western Europe.

The abrupt break-up of the colonial world in the 1950s abruptly made Soviet policy toward the underdeveloped world out of date. Swiftly, what had been colonies took their places in the United Nations as new, politically free and — almost without exception — economically wanting, nations. In this situation as in many other things, Stalin blocked basic change in USSR policy.

After Stalin's death in 1953, Soviet policy toward the underdeveloped areas underwent a dramatic change. It was decided that Marxists should try to make their way to power in the new (and in the still emergent) nations by way of a period of cooperation with the "national bourgeoisie" — the educated class of commerce and the military which had directed (or was directing) revolt against the colonial power, and was the mover and maker of change of all sorts in the new nations. The government of the USSR would establish good official relations with the new ruling class in the former colonies, and would seek to ingratiate itself with the national bourgeoisie of Latin America. Within the new nations, the local Marxist leadership would for a time reduce the clatter of communist unrest to a background noise and would offer help and cooperation in the reorientation of the country's economy and politics resulting from its new status.

The principal instrument for a new approach to the Marxist incursion in the underdeveloped world, Stalin's successors decided, would be the theme of an "alternative to capitalism". The

171

"alternative" was to be materialized in the form of offers of economic and military assistance during and after the "national liberation struggle".

The break up of colonialism that called for new Soviet policy toward the underdeveloped world coincided with the advent of Soviet ability to give assistance. By the mid-1950s Russia had built a large, if second class, industrial establishment. Current agricultural gains provided a feeling of well being. The long concentration in the USSR on investment in the production of capital and military goods had made it possible for Marxist Russia to mass produce many items of military hardware, and many items of industrial capital equipment, especially such things as relatively simple machine tools, at low cost to herself. These could be offered to the new nations as assistance against "neo-colonialism" by the capitalist nations.

Much of the capital goods to be offered was of a relatively low productivity. There were outstanding exceptions, such as the altogether modern steel mill built by the USSR at Bhilai, India. But such equipment could be made available abroad only as an exception, and as a subtraction from capital goods Soviet planners wanted for internal use in Russia. A Soviet planning official, just back from India, lamented in a speech at the June, 1959 meeting of the CPSU's Central Committee in Moscow that high class Soviet equipment, such as he saw in India, was "not common" in Russia.

Most, perhaps all, of the military equipment turned over to the new countries was obsolete (first class military equipment, such as rockets sent to Cuba in 1962, was kept in Russian control). Since Russia was devoting much of her productive energies to keeping her military capabilities and technology on par with those of the United States, she had available for transfer to underdeveloped countries superseded aircraft and other items essentially useless to Russia, and therefore essentially costless.

The vehicle of the "alternative to capitalism", Moscow decided, would be trade. The USSR could not afford to *give* vast amounts of assistance free, as did the United States in its economic and military aid programs for the underdeveloped countries. Consequently, as part of the "alternative to capitalism"

172

concept, USSR assistance was put forth on a "businesslike" basis. Assistance in this form was represented as being more manly — more in keeping with national independence — than the grant aid of the United States.

Manly ring and all, the *quid pro quo* for such assistance could be viewed in the majority of the underdeveloped countries as also being essentially costless, because most of the underdeveloped countries had surplus stocks of the food, fibers, ores, rubber latex and other raw materials the USSR was willing to take in payment.

Both sides to the Soviet aid program could, therefore, put a cost figure on the aid given and received that was small by comparison with the benefits.

The benefits to the USSR would be international prestige; world emergence of Marxist Russia as a producer and dispenser of capital; close acquaintance with an array of nations, containing a major portion of the world's humanity and providing much of the world's raw materials, where Russian influence had always been particularly weak; plus the establishment of bases for the growth of Marxist power inside both the civilian and military establishments of at least some of the new nations.

Russia would receive food, fibers and other raw materials in many cases in short supply in the USSR.

Russia's industry and consumers would both be better supplied, at bargain prices.

The underdeveloped countries would get industrial plant and equipment, military help, laboratories, technical and scientific advice of many kinds, and the like, in return for goods that, by and large, were regarded as surpluses.

Politically, they would get a new string to their bow: the alternative that if they were not treated as they thought they should be by the capitalist world, they could appeal to the Soviet world.

However this may have seemed when looked at from Moscow or, say, from Cairo, looked at from Washington it appeared to be a Soviet economic offensive against the free world, developed and underdeveloped alike.

173

When is Trade
an Economic
Offensive?

During the 1930s the Soviet Union, ragged, unsure and alone, traded such foods as it could coerce from its collectivized peasantry, plus other raw materials, for Western equipment and technology. USSR trade had clear and simple purposes: the swiftest possible industrialization and armament of Soviet Russia. No penetration of the fabric of the free world's economic system was intended or accomplished. The world saw little of the label "Made in the USSR", and when it did see it, took it as notice of probable inferiority. Soviet Russia simply sent to the rest of the world such raw materials as it could wring at lowest cost from its people, by trade converting foods and other primary materials into industrial plant and equipment. The United States was a principal supplier of the USSR's imported technology in the 1930s.

The Communist World was then one nation, communist trade was small, entering only a few markets, taking only a limited range of goods, in deals shunning the light and claiming nothing except that each trade exchange advanced Marxism's strength in Russia. The USSR was the West's client, not its competitor.

The composition of Russia's trade with Europe and Japan, and of her suggestions for expansion of trade with the United States, show that Russia's trade intentions toward the West are the same as ever. Russia is still chiefly interested in technologically seminal imports. She still prefers to be the temporary (as she hopes) *client* of the West, not a *partner* in the free world's trade system of interdependent nations.

What *has* changed, is Soviet trade with the less developed free world.

Since the mid-1950s the expansion of Soviet economic relations with the underdeveloped countries of the free world has been the most dramatic of the . . . developments characterizing total Soviet foreign trade.

174

Until the shift from a defensive to an agressive foreign economic policy, Soviet trade with these areas amounted to only about 5 per cent of total Soviet trade, and to one quarter of Soviet trade with the free world. By 1962, however, trade with these areas had grown to 15 per cent of total trade, and to nearly 45 per cent of Soviet free world trade. The rapid expansion of commodity exchange between the U.S.S.R. and these areas was accompanied by an equally rapid expansion of other contracts—economic, cultural and political.

The number of Soviet technicians working on various developmental projects in underdeveloped countries has grown to nearly 7,000, while the number of students and trainees from these areas in schools or institutes in the U.S.S.R. has similarly mushroomed.

Whole armies have been provided with Soviet military equipment and trained in Soviet military techniques, and delegations of various sorts constantly travel back and forth between the Bloc and the under-developed countries.

All this is very great change. Before the onslaught of the economic offensive, Soviet interest in these areas was probably equally great, but its ability to implement the interest was limited by domestic priorities. Economic contacts were largely confined to commerce, and commerce was primarily the purchase of certain materials—rubber, cotton and wool—for cash.[1]

"Made in the USSR" (and Communist Czechoslovakia, East Germany, Poland, etc.) is now a label seen widely in the world, meant to convey the idea that the Marxist world is helping the free world's poor. In contrast to the sell-and-grab trade, in a few markets only, for a limited range of goods, that has traditionally characterized Marxist trade, Bloc trade now reaches out to the nations of Asia, Latin America, the Middle East and Africa as a program of economic assistance. The orbiter of the first space-man offers to share its ingenuity. The only military power near par with the United States offers to share its armaments and knowledge. The management of the world's second biggest in-dustrial complex offers to share its technology and capital goods.

There is, here, an active intent to penetrate the fabric of the economies with which the USSR is trading in the underdeveloped areas. Trade with the underdeveloped countries is trade involv-

[1] Penelope H. Thunberg in *Dimensions of Soviet Economic Power*, p. 433.

ing indebtedness to, and by, the USSR, within the framework of trade agreements running years ahead. These long term arrangements, involving such important staples as, for instance, Cuba's sugar and Egypt's cotton, alter the flow of the world's economic resources, shunting them away from lines established over long periods of time by the growth of industry and markets in the industrialized nations of the West. The Soviet trade with the underdeveloped countries is offered as competition to Western institutions, goods, services, practices and markets. It calls itself assistance of a better, more disinterested, character than the much greater aid given by the West, chiefly by the United States (see Table 17). It is trade-as-aid.

The Soviet trade drive in the underdeveloped free world is an economic offensive in two senses.

It is an offensive in the same sense as is any sales campaign: it seeks to enter new markets, to reduce the share of business going to competitors, to establish new commercial allegiances and channels, to change existing ideas and images concerning goods and services, to move toward future expansion and tighter contact. In this strictly competitive sense, the United States could have no legitimate objection to the expansion of USSR trade with the underdeveloped free world countries.

The unacceptably offensive characteristic of the USSR trade drive lies in the same — competition shunning — one way view of change that we have noted as the distinguishing feature of Marxist Russia's world outlook as a whole. The USSR seeks to "compete" economically only until Marxism has gained the upper hand. At that point, competition is to be closed down, and exclusive arangements (such as those in Comecon) between the newly Marxist nation and the Soviet world are to take over. This is military-political, not economic competition: it seeks to penetrate so as to ingest.

The complete redirection of the economies of the East European countries that fell under the Red Army during World War II illustrates the process. More recently, the complete reorientation of Cuba's economy toward the Bloc demonstrates the continuing effects of the one way policy. These examples of one way change compare very badly with the liberation of the Asian-

176

African colonial world, which at the end of World War II was under European control, and to the development and liberation of the Philippines, and Cuba, under the United States. In the free world the idea has been accepted that change may run against, as well as for, the dominant power.[1]

In controlling Russian Marxist thought, as well as in current example, Russian Marxism continued to insist upon its "law governed" right to gain power by revolution (violent or otherwise, as convenient) and guide nations so recruited toward a "higher" destiny under Marxism. This was reaffirmed in 1961 in the CPSU's New Program:

> The Socialist world is expanding, the capitalist world is shrinking. Socialism will inevitably succeed capitalism everywhere. Such is the objective law of social development. . . .

> Whatever the form in which the transition from capitalism to socialism is effected, that transition can come about only through revolution. However varied the forms of a new, people's state power . . . their essence will be the same—dictatorship of the proletariat, which represents genuine democracy . . .[2]

*The Soviet
Economic Offensive —
A Profile*

The economic offensive by the USSR and other Bloc countries got under way in 1954, with an $11 million credit by Russia to her strategically placed neighbor Afghanistan. Through 1962, the drive to lodge Marxist influence in the underdeveloped countries of the free world had resulted in commitment of credits

---

[1]Cuba is probably a net economic burden to the USSR. What seems to have happened there is the acceptance by Russia (by no means as generously as Cuba would have liked) of responsibility for Cuba's needs for economic assistance in return for Cuba's military assistance to Russia. Cuba could become a military outpost for Russia in no other way, because the United States was certain to cut off its trade lines with Cuba when Cuba became a rocket base for the USSR. Subsequently, Russia had to reaffirm its intention to substitute Comecon trade with Cuba for Cuba's lost US trade because Cuba became a key piece in a struggle between Russia and Red China for Marxist primacy in Latin America. In 1964 Russia appeared to be trying to ease this burden— since the military gain was uncertain—by reducing the USSR military presence in Cuba and encouraging Castro to seek a renewal of trade relations with the US. Castro appeared reluctant to make the indispensable move—renunciation of his role as Chief Revolutionary throughout Latin America.

[2]*New York Times,* August 1, 1961.

(and a few grants) amounting to just under $7 billion for economic and military assistance combined.

Of this, some $4.3 billion was economic assistance. The USSR contributed $3¼ billion of total Bloc economic assistance. Table 17 outlines Sino-Soviet Bloc, USSR and United States aid since 1945. There was no Bloc aid before 1954. *Total* United States aid is given in totals for the free world, for areas and for the world. United States aid *by country* is shown only to countries that have also received Bloc aid. This permits comparison of total United States, Bloc and USSR aid by areas, and in countries where the Bloc has been active.

Through 1962, the underdeveloped countries had been able, or willing, to draw upon only 30 per cent of the Bloc credits committed to them for economic assistance. That is, they had actually received Soviet goods and services, or were in the process of doing so, amounting to about $1.3 billion. All military aid committed had been used.[1]

The USSR is the source of somewhat over 70 per cent of Bloc economic aid, Russia's Eastern European allies account for about 22 per cent, and Red China for about 8 per cent. (This makes Red Chinese economic assistance to underdeveloped free world nations approximately $350 million. Chinese assistance went to her neighbors in southern Asia. Not only is Red China a bottomless pit of need, there is a politically motivated drain away from the pit.)

By comparison with United States aid, USSR aid is very small. This continues to be the case if we add to USSR economic aid to free world underdeveloped countries its economic assistance to Bloc countries, and adjust the totals for the relative sizes of the United States and USSR economies. See table on following page.

Without adjustment for the size of gross national product, USSR commitments for economic assistance to all countries in the postwar years 1945-1962 comes to nearly 15 per cent of total United States economic aid. Adjusting it according to the difference in the size of Russia's economy, and ours, (to show relative aid *efforts* by the two countries, considering their eco-

[1] See footnotes to Table 17 for sources of data used in this section.

nomic strength) raises Soviet economic aid commitments close to a third of United States economic aid commitments to all countries. In 1963 the USSR was known to have made new economic aid commitments to free world countries of $168 million. In the same year, new United States economic aid commitments came to $5.0 billion.

USSR and
United States
Economic Aid
1945-1962

USSR aid commitments to free world underdeveloped countries .... $ 3.2 billion[1]
USSR aid to communist countries .... $ 6.6 billion[2]
Total USSR assistance, 1945-62 .... $ 9.8 billion
US GNP = 2.15 times USSR GNP (see Table 1)
USSR economic assistance multiplied by 2.15 .... $21.1 billion
Total US economic assistance, 1945-62 .... $66.5 billion[3]

[1] About 30 per cent disbursed through 1962.
[2] Includes, as aid, cancellation of debts to the USSR.
[3] About 45 per cent disbursed through 1962.

However, difficulties with Bloc deliveries, probably combined with reluctance by some underdeveloped countries to increase their international indebtedness under the nearly all-credit, no-grant Bloc aid program, held actual usage of Bloc aid to only 30 per cent of commitments through 1962. Applying this to USSR assistance would indicate that the actual drain on the USSR economy for help to the free world underdeveloped countries, 1954-62, was only about $1 billion. Since intra-Bloc assistance credits are apparently used quickly, this would suggest that total USSR *output* for assistance to all countries through 1962 was not above $7.6 billion. Some 45 per cent of United States economic aid commitments — or $30 billion — was used from 1945 through 1962.

Although United States assistance has been less than Bloc or USSR aid to some African countries (Guinea, Mali and Somali Republic), the United States has given over two and a half times more help to Africa, all told, than has the Bloc, and four times the USSR total. In Africa, both Bloc and United States aid programs date from about 1954.

The United States has made by far its biggest effort, since 1954, in Asia, and after that Latin America and the Middle East

179

have had large shares. The Bloc and the USSR have done little in Latin America, except in Cuba (where Bloc aid was mainly military through 1962). But four tenths of Bloc and USSR aid commitments to the free world have gone to Asia. The United States invested 45 per cent of its 1954-62 aid commitments in the free world underdeveloped countries of Asia. The United States put 14 per cent of its aid effort into the Middle East during the years 1954-62 after the Bloc economic assistance program began, while 37 per cent of Bloc assistance went to the Middle East and Russia invested 44 per cent of its free world aid in the Middle East.

The Bloc assistance program concentrated very heavily on a few countries. Of the total $4.3 billion of Bloc economic aid committed to free world underdeveloped countries, almost two thirds went to: two countries in Asia (India, 22 per cent and Indonesia, 15 per cent) together with two countries in the Middle East (Afghanistan, 12 per cent and Egypt, 16 per cent).

The only country to get more than 10 per cent of United States economic aid from 1954 through 1962 was India, which received nearly 12 per cent. India was also the country which has received the most Bloc economic aid (heavily USSR). Pakistan, Brazil and Turkey are the other countries upon which United States aid has focused.

The countries where United States and Bloc assistance met, 1954-62, in large scale competition (beginning at about $100 million economic aid from each side) were Argentina, Afghanistan, Egypt, Ethiopia, Ghana, India, Indonesia, Syria and Yugoslavia. Grants constitute about 5½ per cent of Bloc aid ($236 million out of $4.34 billion).

Loans thus make up over 94 per cent of all Bloc aid. In the 1954-62 period, after the Bloc program began, 53 per cent of United States aid ($16.0 billion out of $30.4 billion) was in the form of grants. Only in 1961 and 1962 did United States assistance become more than one half credits. Bloc and United States credits tend to take about the same form on the average, and to be available at about the same rates of interest and on similar repayment terms. In both cases, there have been wide variations from what came to be the norms. Over the years, Bloc terms have tended to tighten somewhat, and United States terms to loosen.

Bloc assistance is almost entirely directed to single projects, sometime large, but often small. United States aid generally takes the form of assistance to a broad inter-connected band of industrial, agricultural and institutional projects all of which are intended to form, together, a coherent program of economic development in the nation concerned. Bloc aid commitments through 1962 were 57 per cent directed at industrial projects. The rest was scattered over single, unassociated projects to improve transportation, communication, technical schools, mineral exploration and exploitation, reclamation, irrigation, hydroelectric power, health and other municipal services and credits for commodities.

Excluding the military situation in Cuba, some 10,000 Bloc technicians and advisers, (military and civilian) were working in 30 underdeveloped free world countries at the end of 1962. Several thousand citizens of the underdeveloped countries were studying or training in the communist countries.

Trade is
Aid,
to Whom?

The USSR and the Bloc have been trading on an increasing scale with the underdeveloped nations of the free world since 1954. The trade arises almost completely from trade agreements represented as economic development assistance to the underdeveloped countries.

Table 15 shows USSR trade for the years 1955-62. This indicates that in the eight years through 1962 Soviet Russia was able to import some $1 billion more from the underdeveloped countries than she exported to them. (In this table the standard practice of indicating a surplus of exports with a favorable, or plus, sign and a surplus of imports with an unfavorable, or minus, sign was followed). That is, Russia *received* net assistance in terms of economic resources exchanged. In no year did Russian exports to the underdeveloped free world countries equal imports.

To the extent balances were settled in gold or convertible currencies, there was no net advantage to one side or the other. But, as we saw in the preceding section, the USSR and her allies in the Communist West are chronically short of foreign exchange. They only reluctantly settle accounts with the underdeveloped countries in gold or convertible money, because they need the exchange reserves for trade with industrialized countries. It is the practice of the Bloc countries to carry over and renegotiate trade balances up to, at least, $10 million. Judging by the large number of countries involved in making up these balances, many of the year-end balances would have been carried over, permitting the USSR to receive economic assistance, since she took in (imported) more economic resources than she sent out (exported).

Table 18 spreads the record for the whole Bloc for the nine years 1954-62. In this table, the trade exchanges are looked at as they would appear to the Bloc planner calculating the economic resources at his disposal. In this view, an outflow of economic resources (exports) is a subtraction from available economic resources, and an inflow of resources (imports) is an addition to economic resources available for use. Consequently, *minus* signs appear on Bloc export surpluses, and *plus* signs on Bloc import surpluses, the reverse of the usual practice.

By this different accounting, for the first nine years of the trade offensive the USSR stood to *gain* by a net inflow of resources from the underdeveloped free world amounting to nearly three quarters of a billion dollars. In no part of the underdeveloped free world did USSR exports equal USSR imports.

The European Bloc countries exported somewhat more than they imported in trade with the underdeveloped countries, leaving the Communist West the gainer by over half a billion dollars for the nine years.

Red China gave up a net of about $1.5 billion worth of goods in its trade with underdeveloped free world countries during this period. Due almost entirely to the large Red China export surplus, the communist world as a whole gave assistance to the underdeveloped countries, in the form of economic resources exchanged, of nearly one billion dollars, from 1954-62. But the USSR *received* about three fourths of a billion dollars help, in the form of an inflow of economic resources, from the under-developed countries.

The
Commodity
Problem

It is doubtful if the USSR and her allies in the Communist West could have carried out their economic offensive against the free world except for the existence of a single outstanding free world economic problem: chronic surpluses of the foods, fibers and minerals which are the chief stock in trade of the under-developed countries, and excessive dependence of most of these countries on trade in one, or a very few, of the primary commodities.

This is the commodity problem.

A recent study for the United States Senate described the problem:

> The export of primary commodities is the very core of the economies of the underdeveloped countries. These commodities account for 25 per cent or more of the total national output of goods and services, and virtually 100 per cent of exports. Producing and selling for export, often of just one or two commodities, has even greater importance to many countries than corn has to Iowa, coal to West Virginia, or rubber to Akron. Nothing escapes the good or bad fortune of the commodity markets.

> Consider employment and income. In a country such as El Salvador the largest crop, coffee, constitutes about 90 per cent of exports. More farmhands are engaged tending coffee trees than in working on any other product. Still others process the coffee, transport it to market, and load it aboard ship. The expenditures made by the farm hands, their employers, and the merchants engaged in coffee production mean that the banker, the shopkeepers, and virtually all other businesses are dependent on the income of those engaged in producing coffee for export.

> This is equally true in Haiti and in many other coffee-producing countries in Latin America and Africa; for the tin-producing countries of Malaya and Bolivia; for the copper countries of Chile and Rhodesia; for the rice countries of Burma and Thailand . . .

183

Government operations are also seriously affected by the commodity export situation. Most Government revenues derive from what are, effectively, taxes on exports and from duties on imports paid for through export earnings. Together, these imports may account for 90 per cent of all government revenues. When exports fall or fail to grow, governments cannot finance vital activities including economic development projects.

The savings which finance these development projects are also largely derived from exports. Profits made in the production and sale for export are the largest source of savings in many countries. Investment funds dry up when earnings from commodities fall.

The pressure on export earnings directly affects trade relations with Iron Curtain countries. Increasingly, the Soviet Union and its satellites are offering to buy surplus primary products.[1]

Other studies of the commodity problem said:

The countries of Latin America must import most of the capital equipment they need for their development. They must pay for these imports with earnings from their exports or with the proceeds of borrowing, which in turn must be serviced with export earnings. An upward trend of export earnings and reasonable stability around the trend are essential to the economic growth of Latin America.[2]

The problem of many less developed countries in disposing of their principal export commodities in traditional markets at prices they consider satisfactory provides the Bloc with opportunities to exploit trade relations as a tool of diplomacy. The Bloc thus has taken advantage of Burma's temporary rice surplus, Egypt's cotton disposal problem, Uruguay's wool production, and Iceland's difficulty in marketing fish, and it has thereby been able to expand its relations with these countries.[3]

The USSR takes advantage of the commodity problem of the free world by the "Kind Uncle Phenomenon": a small boy

---

[1] *The United States and World Trade,* Special Staff on the study of US Foreign Commerce, Committee on Interstate and Foreign Commerce, US Senate, March, 1961. The underdeveloped countries held a special world conference on their problems beginning at Geneva, early in 1964. One of the main efforts of the conference was to draw attention to the commodity problem and get special trade concessions and trade arrangements, from the developed countries, to overcome it.

[2] *Cooperation for Progress in Latin America,* a Statement on National Policy by the Research and Policy Committee, Committee for Economic Development, New York, April, 1963, p. 26.

[3] *Communist Economic Policy in the Less Developed Areas,* Department of State Publication 7020, July, 1960, p. 22.

184

gets his food, lodging, shelter, clothing and all the rest from his parents, as usual; but the small boy has a kind uncle, who drops by now and then and buys the boy a piece of candy, or takes him to a movie; the uncle, not the boy's parents, is the boy's ideal of generosity and solicitude.

The West (and Japan) buy over 90 per cent of all the foods, fibers and minerals produced for export by the underdeveloped countries of the free world. The Soviet Union and the rest of the Bloc take substantially less than 10 per cent.[1] Upon this small fraction of the total trade of the underdeveloped countries, the Soviet Union has built its economic offensive against the West.

It is clear that playing anything other than the Kind Uncle, the USSR (or the Bloc) would be disastrously inadequate as a market for the underdeveloped countries. But so long as the underdeveloped countries continue to have markets for over nine tenths of their exports in the capitalist countries, the USSR and its allies can continue to operate their economic offensive on the margin of world commodity markets, picking up moral and political credits, as well as welcome amounts of foods and raw materials, in exchange for the Communist West's limited amounts of expendable capital goods and less limited but less useful military equipment. A few highly strategic exceptions, such as India, Indonesia, Afghanistan and Egypt (and perhaps Cuba) could continue to receive exceptional assistance, but this, as Cuba learned, tends to be strictly limited.

Leon Herman, of the Legislative Reference Service, Library of Congress, set the problem out in general form:

> As a practical matter, the foreign economic resources of the Soviet camp can scarcely be qualified as a plausible "alternative." Because of their built-in institutional commitment to autarky, internal as well as intrabloc, the Communist countries do not have much to spare for trade with the outside world. Taken together, all Communist lands contribute only $4.2 billion to the total volume of goods flowing through the channels of world trade. In 1961, total world trade was measured

---

[1] Table 3 C, 15th Report to Congress, Mutual Defense Assistance Control Act of 1951, Department of State Publication 7230, March, 1962, indicates the Bloc took 5.1 per cent of trade of the underdeveloped free world countries in 1959, and perhaps as much as 7.7 per cent in 1960. According to the United Nations *Monthly Bulletin of Statistics* for June, 1963, this fell to 6.7 per cent in 1962.

by an export figure of $118 billion.[1]

In direct contrast, the developing nations are very much involved in the activities of the world market. Like it or not, most of them are, by their very nature, export economies. They do not, and cannot, live in isolation. As a group, they sell currently some $28 billion of commodities in the world market. Of this total, the share of the Soviet bloc as a whole comes to only 4.3 per cent. The proportion is roughly the same on the import side; only 4.1 per cent of the $30 billion worth of goods imported by the less developed countries in 1961 came from the Sino-Soviet group of nations.

In the field of trade, the prime objective of the newly developing nations is to employ their export resources in such a way as to help speed up their economic development. To this end, they try to maximize the import of industrial equipment in the course of any one year. Here, too, the preponderant source is the capitalist market. In 1960 the industrialized countries of the West delivered to the underdeveloped countries a quantity of equipment valued at $7.6 billion. In contrast, imports in this category from the Soviet bloc amounted to less than $300 million, in the same year.[2]

The USSR
as a Development
Model

The Soviet economy was planned not for the harmony of its different branches, but for one single purpose, namely the most rapid industrialization and preparation of effective national defense. . . . Soviet economic planning did not serve the objectives of a harmonious socialist welfare economy, but served political and military objectives to which all other aspects of economic planning were sacrificed.

The above is the view of the USSR economy of one of Marxism's foremost and least orthodox thinkers, the Polish philosopher-economist Oskar Lange.[3] It emphasizes, on the basis

[1] By 1962 the Bloc share rose slightly, since total Bloc contribution to world trade was $4.7 billion and total world trade was $124 billion.

[2] Leon Herman, *Dimensions of Soviet Economic Power:* pp. 483-484.

[3] *USSR Economy and the War,* Russian Economic Institute, (now defunct), New York, 1943, p. 43.

Bibliographical Note: Suggested further reading on this subject would include: "A Model for Underdeveloped Countries?" in *The Soviet Economy,* by Alec Nove, (George Allen and Unwin, Ruskin House, London), 1961; Alex Inkeles and Oleg Hoeffding, "The Soviet Union, Model for Asia?" in *Problems of Communism,* Vol. VIII, No. 6, December, 1959; Francis Seton, "Planning and Economic Growth," *Soviet Survey,* No. 31, March, 1960; the "Introduction" to *Survey,* No. 38, October, 1961; *The Chinese Communes;* and United Nations, *World Economic Survey, 1961,* Introduction and Part I.

of intimate knowledge of Soviet Russia's Marxism, what has often come to the surface in this study: that the overriding drive in the USSR is the build-up, and protection, of an industrial-military complex, to serve Soviet Russia's need to be foremost in the Communist world as a base for Russia's drive for world hegemony.

Countries that do not have such ambitions, but are seeking development chiefly so that their people may live better lives, must question the Soviet economic development model in all its aspects.

We have seen that as a trade partner, the USSR takes more from the underdeveloped country than it gives in return (Tables 15 and 18). We have also seen that there is very little to export for economic development from the Socialist Nations System: Russia comes first, and must be nourished best and most; after Russia come her partners and supporters in Eastern Europe; Communist China and her fellows in misery in the Communist East come last, if they are helped at all. We noted in Part I that since a considerable qualitative lead over her fellow communist nations is a condition of continued USSR dominance of world Marxism, a growing discrepancy between Russian development and the development of others in the Bloc is to be expected. Underdeveloped nations entering the Bloc should note that their place may be near the bottom of the list, as a Bloc member, although they were high on the priority list as free world nations.

But:

One of the more important ways in which Soviet ideas exercise an influence on people in the uncommitted world is through the quite widespread belief that the USSR — and perhaps China too — demonstrates how it is possible rapidly to transform a peasant country into a great industrial power.[1]

If the USSR *is* a good model in this respect, it is a matter of the highest importance for the underdeveloped countries because it is indeed the outstanding fact of economic development for most of the less developed countries that their problem is to shift from agriculture to industry. The United Nations' *World Economic Survey, 1961* found that:

---

[1] Alec Nove, "A Model for Underdeveloped Countries?" in *The Soviet Economy*.

In the present day, primary production accounts, on the average, for about 47 per cent of total domestic output in the lowest-income countries, while industry contributes slightly less than 20 per cent. By contrast, in the high-income industrial countries, these proportions are quite the reverse. . . .

The poorer the country, the more this is so, according to data in the UN study, seen in Table 20.

The first question about the validity of the Soviet development model should be, was Russia just before communism about like an underdeveloped country of today? It appears that Russia was deriving about a fifth of its national income from industry in 1913. This would place it among the underdeveloped countries according to the UN data cited just above. However, at that time, Russia was the fifth or sixth country in the world in overall industrialization (the fourth ranking in production of machinery and textiles). This made her much stronger in relation to her contemporaries than today's country getting only a fifth of its income from industry. There is evidence that the Russian savings rate was high and rising in 1913 and that its growth rate was high — around 5 per cent. That is, Russia had a strong industrial base, investment funds were accumulating rapidly, and industry was already growing fast. This is not the picture of a country in pastoral-traditional doldrums.

> Russia in 1913 was clearly ahead of both India and China at the outset of their respective first Five Year Plans, and therefore very far ahead of any other Asian country, save Japan.[1]

But the biggest difference between Russia at the outset of Communism and the underdeveloped country of today was probably agricultural output. Adam Smith said:

> It is the surplus produce of the country only, or *what is over and above the maintenance of the cultivators,* that constitutes the subsistence of the town, which can therefore increase only with the increase of the surplus produce.[2]

Russia had "surplus produce of the country" when communization began, because Russian agriculture had been undergoing

---

[1] Oleg Hoeffding, "State Planning and Forced Industrialization," *Problems of Communism,* Vol. VIII, No. 6.

[2] *Wealth of Nations,* Book III, Chapter 1, emphasis supplied.

some modernization since the late 19th Century. As one of the many signs of this, Russia in 1913 exported 9 million tons of grains. Further, Russia was in position to add to her agricultural output by bringing more land under cultivation as her population increased. Russia had 1.1 hectares of cultivated land per head of population in 1913 and the same in 1956.[1]

Russia had a fairly thin population in 1913, and was not faced with a fast rising population during the period of industrial growth under communism. Russia in 1960 had only about 50 million more people than in 1913; India expects to add 50 million people to her population during the present decade, and many other free world underdeveloped countries have rates of increase as high as India's.[1]

In all these basic respects, communism got a much better start in Russia than it would get in most of the underdeveloped countries of today. In this study we have seen that Russia has become the second most powerful economy in the world. *But we have noted as a basic finding that everywhere in the Marxist world, in Russia and in other communist countries that have tried to pursue the Russian development strategy, a great flaw has developed: a profound economic imbalance caused by agricultural stagnation under Marxism.* Agricultural deficiency resulting from agricultural stagnation now threatens everywhere in the socialist nations system to command a pause in industrial growth, and, if it is not quickly corrected, threatens to develop into an absolute limit upon economic growth and refinement under Marxism.

Soviet Russia has been a fast growing economy, but it has not become a low cost, or high productivity economy, and its growth is slowing down. One of the chief reasons is the drag upon it of its agricultural deficiency. Few of the free world underdeveloped countries have so low a ratio of population to economic resources that they can afford a development policy that does not have at its center a high level of agricultural efficiency.

Even as respects industry only, there is a question whether the Soviet example is the best one for the underdeveloped countries, particularly those with dense populations.

---

[1] Hoeffding, *Problems of Communism*, op. cit.

It is of course logical to argue that in conditions of open or disguised unemployment, expansion of large-scale highly capitalized industries would add to the number of idle hands. But it is also demonstrable that it is the large-scale heavy industries that are the vehicles of technological progress.

What then is the way out of the dilemma? A leaf can be taken here from the Japanese rather than the Soviet book.

The Soviet Union prides herself on the biggest concentration of large-scale industry; plants employing more than 1,000 workers account for well over three-fifths of total industrial manpower. In contrast, Japan holds the world record among industrial nations for the share of small scale industry. Enterprises with fewer than 50 employees absorb half of the gainfully employed.[1]

Red China's disasters and frustrations trying to follow the Russian path of economic development are an object lesson. What they show particularly is that where the agricultural surplus that Adam Smith singled out as the ineludible basis for development is lacking, it must be supplied before much else can be done. And if *much* is to be done by way of industrial development, agricultural efficiency must constantly be raised (through investment in agricultural education, capital equipment, fertilizer production or import, and the like) so that a constant stream of manpower is released for employment in industry, and so this manpower, once in the city, can be fed cheaply and supplied cheaply with industrial raw materials.

It is not our business in this concluding section to try to do more than raise some of the principal questions about the USSR as a model for economic growth. The subject of the sources of economic growth, and the correct approach to the activation of those sources is one of the most debated questions of the times.[2] However, it would appear to be beyond any doubt that the Russian Marxist model of economic growth is a model with a starting point unavailable to most underdeveloped countries, and with objectives foreign to the requirements of most, if not all of them. Further, to cater to its military-political ambitions, Russian Marx-

---

[1] Alfred Zauberman in *The Chinese Communes*.

[2] For a view of what is known about growth factors, see Edward F. Denison, *The Sources of Economic Growth in the United States and the Alternatives Before Us,* Supplementary Paper No. 13, Committee for Economic Development, New York, 1962.

ist development policy accepted agricultural stagnation and further accepted a commitment to maximum output of selected strategic goods, regardless of cost. Few of the underdeveloped countries have the agricultural surplus that would permit them to follow very far down this Russian road — witness China— without experiencing large scale disaster. Few, if any, have Russia's military-political reasons for industrialization on a cost-be-damned basis.

Red China has developed an approach to economic development that appears to be more realistic in the circumstances of most underdeveloped countries than is Russia's. But Chinese policy is touched, or utterly dominated, by the same world power megalomania as sits at the center of Soviet policy. (One of Mao Tse-tung's favorite, and most applied, aphorisms is that "Power grows out of the mouth of a gun".) So Chinese development policy may depart from current realism at the first opportunity, leaving in the lurch countries looking for a practical Marxist model for economic development *per se*.

Beyond these questions with their roots in the technicalities of economics lie greater, qualitative questions about the Soviet model. They are questions centering upon the query, What is Russian Marxism aiming to accomplish? We will take as our answer a passage from the introduction by the editors of *Survey* to the issue of their journal analyzing the Third Program — New Program, as we have called it here — of the Communist Party of the Soviet Union.[1]

> What will Soviet society accomplish? . . . Even if there should be a gradual transformation of the totalitarian state into a relatively enlightened authoritarian regime . . . will the regime have justified its cost in human suffering and sacrifice? If all the high hopes, the great efforts, and the idealism have only produced a system with somewhat greater rates of economic growth, and considerably more repression than other industrialized nations, it will be interesting to know how its proponents will explain its *raison d'etre*. We may have to wait for the fourth programme for an answer.

The Fourth Program may have to explain, first of all, why Marxist growth rates, to say nothing of progress toward a more liberal society, did not remain exceptionally high.

---

[1] *Survey,* No. 38.